IMAGINATIVE PRAYER
FOR YOUTH MI

A GUIDE TO TRANSFORMING YOUR STUDENTS' SPIRITUAL LIVES INTO JOURNEY, ADVENTURE, AND ENCOUNTER

D0764528

JEANNIE OESTREICHER & LARRY WARNER

ZONDERVAN®

Youth Specialties
.com

ZONDERVAN.com/
AUTHORTRACKER
follow your favorite authors

Imaginative Prayer for Youth Ministry
Copyright ©2006 by Jeannie Oestreicher and Larry Warner

Youth Specialties Books, 300 S. Pierce St., El Cajon, CA 92020 are published by Zondervan, 5300 Patterson Ave. SE, Grand Rapids, MI 49530.

Library of Congress Cataloging-in-Publication Data

Oestreicher, Jeannie.
  Imaginative prayer for youth ministry / Jeannie Oestreicher and Larry
Warner.
     p. cm.
  Includes indexes.
  ISBN-10: 0-310-27094-4
  ISBN-13: 978-0-310-27094-2
  1. Youth--Religious life. 2. Prayer--Christianity. 3. Church work with
youth. I. Warner, Larry, 1955- II. Title.
  BV4531.3.O37 2006
  259'.23--dc22

                                                                                   2006020360

This edition printed on acid-free paper.

Any Web site addresses listed in this book were current at the time of publication. Please contact Youth Specialties via e-mail (YS@YouthSpecialties.com) to report URLs that are no longer operational and replacement URLs if available.

Creative Team: Dave Urbanski, Laura Gross, Heather Haggerty, Rich Cairnes, Mark Novelli/ IMAGO MEDIA
Cover design by SharpSeven Design

Printed in the United States of America

06 07 08 09 10 11 12 • 23 22 21 20 19 18 17 16 15 14 13 12 11 10 9 8 7 6 5 4 3 2 1

Jeannie: To the one I love most, my husband and partner, Mark.

Larry: To Donna, my lovely and beautiful friend, wife, and lover these last 27-plus years.

ACKNOWLEDGMENTS

We are grateful to many people who have helped make this book a possibility. To Marko, you initially encouraged this book idea and kept encouraging all along the way. To Jay, thank you for buying in so quickly and working to sell the idea to others. To Laura, your early encouragement and assistance gave us added confidence, and your back-end efforts are much appreciated! Dave, thank you for gently helping us make this a better book than it might have been. The YS/Zondervan team, you've shown us newbies lots of grace and patience. We thank you.

A special thanks to Marv, both for writing a significant sidebar and your energetic encouragement of our ideas and hopes. Your enthusiasm was pivotal in cementing our own value of this project for youth ministry.

Mindi, Will, Renee, Paul, Lisa, Jerilyn, and Celia, you lent us ideas, feedback, and expertise. Thank you. We are grateful for your generous help and friendship.

Jeannie's acknowledgments: Mark, thank you for the beautiful balance you offered—letting my book be mine and yet being fully available for input and encouragement. I believed I could do this because I believed you when you told me so. Liesl, my sweet girl, thank you for giving me ideas for my book and thank you for letting me practice some of my imaginative prayer meditations on you! You're a great sport. Max, you are awesome! You let me sit in front of my computer for lots of hours. Thank you—that was a really big present you gave me.

Larry, thank you for exposing me to imaginative prayer and for inviting me into such beautiful interactions with God. You inspired the idea for this book, and I'm extremely grateful that you chose to partner with me on this project. Although it wasn't a Dick Van Dyke episode every day, the process was enriching and has definitely left me smiling.

Larry's acknowledgments: Jeannie, thanks for believing enough in the value of imaginative prayer for youth ministry to submit the idea to YS and for believing enough in me to invite me to join you on this adventure in writing. Your belief, courage, and hard work turned a dream into a reality, and your invitation to partner with you is a gift beyond measure. It has been an honor and joy to journey with you in the writing of this book.

Stephanie, Mickey, Nathan, and Ricky, you have each taught me things about myself and God—things that have molded and shaped me into the person I am today. Watching you each step out into your various life adventures has given me more courage to step out and try my hand at new and scary things. This book flows from our life together—a life of change, adventure, heartache, love, and faith. I am proud to be your dad.

TOP 10 REASONS TO USE IMAGINATIVE PRAYER IN YOUTH MINISTRY

1. It's not the same old programmatic youth group idea.

2. It's old! But in a good way—it has stood the test of time. Imagination is encouraged both in Scripture and in early church history.

3. God created imagination; so using it to connect with God is a good thing.

4. It can break down the walls we build to protect us from our own feelings.

5. It's prayer. What youth worker doesn't want their kids to pray?

6. It can help students experience God.

7. It's usually quiet.

8. It lets youth workers get creative.

9. God speaks to people through their imaginations.

10. Students can see, hear, feel, touch, and taste that God is good when they use their imaginations.

CONTENTS

THREE (COUNT 'EM—THREE!) INTRODUCTIONS   9

Take your pick...

SECTION 1—WHY?

CHAPTER 1: OUR STORIES   14

The authors' personal experiences with imaginative prayer

CHAPTER 2: BEGINNINGS   19

The legitimacy of imaginative prayer according to the Bible, church history, and contemporary Christian thinkers and writers

CHAPTER 3: CONCERNS AND RESPONSES   24

Acknowledges and explores common objections to and concerns about imaginative prayer

SECTION 2—HOW?

CHAPTER 4: ANY TAKERS?   28

Helping you consider whether or not imaginative prayer is a good option for your ministry

CHAPTER 5: DEVELOPING THE ENVIRONMENT   32

Input and ideas for maximizing the physical and emotional environment

CHAPTER 6: THE BASICS   40

How to actually facilitate imaginative prayer exercises (and what you need to keep in mind)

SECTION 3—WHAT?

Fifty imaginative prayer exercises, complete with instructions, thoughts about making the most of your physical environment during the exercises, verbatim meditations, and optional debriefing questions.

CHAPTER 7: IMAGES OF GOD

God as Eagle	52
God as Mother	54
God as Potter	55
God as Rescuer	57
God as Shepherd	59

CHAPTER 8: O.T. TIME

God Sees Hagar	61
Hannah's Cry	63
Elijah Rests and Eats	64
God Whispers to Elijah	67
Esther's Courage	68
The Desperate Cry	70
A New Name	72
Daniel and the Lions' Den	73

CHAPTER 9: GOSPEL TIME—ADVENT

Mary's Pregnant	76
Shepherds in the Field	78

CHAPTER 10: GOSPEL TIME

Names (Images) of Jesus	80
God with Us	83
The Lord's Prayer	85
"I Never Knew You"	88
Rest	90
"Who Do You Say I Am?" (Jesus)	93
"Who Do You Say I Am?" (Us)	96
Coming to Jesus	98
Woman with the Alabaster Jar	100
Good Samaritan	102
Martha	103
The Prodigal	105
John's Disciple Follows Jesus	108
Woman Caught in Adultery	110
Death of Lazarus	113

CHAPTER 11: GOSPEL TIME — MIRACLES

Jesus Walks on Water   115
Peter Walks on Water   117
Jesus Calms the Storm   120
Resting with Jesus   122
She Touches His Robe   125
The Blind Beggar   127
Healing the Leper   129
Resurrection of Lazarus   132

CHAPTER 12: GOSPEL TIME — HOLY WEEK

Foot Washing   134
Garden of Gethsemane   136
The Crucifixion   138

CHAPTER 13: N.T. TIME

Peter and Cornelius   142
Temple of God   144

CHAPTER 14: BEYOND THE NARRATIVE

Blanket Walk   146
Bubbles   148
The Feast   150
The Letter   152
Playing in the Leaves with Dad   155
Hide-and-Seek   157
Sunrise   160

APPENDIX

Get Creative! More Imaginative Prayer Ideas   163

ADDITIONAL RESOURCES

169

INDEX BY SCRIPTURE REFERENCE

170

INDEX BY THEME

174

THREE (COUNT 'EM—THREE!) INTRODUCTIONS

> THE SOUL WITHOUT IMAGINATION IS WHAT AN
> OBSERVATORY WOULD BE WITHOUT A TELESCOPE.
>
> —*HENRY WARD BEECHER (1813-1887),*
> *AMERICAN PREACHER, ORATOR, WRITER*

Imaginative prayer can help bring us face-to-face with the God of the universe and the God of our hearts. It can help bridge the abyss that exists between head knowledge and heart experience. And we all want to help our students jump across that abyss.

This book exists because over and over again we've seen imaginative prayer act as a bridge. We've observed students and adults experience the transformational impact of seeing, hearing, tasting, and feeling truths in deeper ways through imaginative prayer. We wanted to share this prayer practice with youth workers, hoping you and your students will find it as significant and meaningful as we have.

While sitting at a coffeehouse, we thought about how to introduce this book. We wanted to speak to each of you; so we've written three intros, hoping you'll find one that fits you.

Here's how it works: First, read each of the three initial statements—hopefully you'll find one that describes where you are with imaginative prayer.

- "I'm so excited to find a book on this! I love imaginative prayer."—Intro One

- "What is imaginative prayer? Speak slowly, please."—Intro Two

- "Combining the words *imagination* and *prayer* makes me nervous. It doesn't sound entirely Christian."—Intro Three

Then skip ahead and read the introduction that follows your chosen statement. It will describe what this book is about, and it may also help you decide whether or not you want to keep reading.

INTRO ONE: "I'M SO EXCITED TO FIND A BOOK ON THIS! I LOVE IMAGINATIVE PRAYER."

We do, too! Imaginative prayer has impacted our lives, both in how we see ourselves and how we see God. In addition, it's been wonderful to lead others in imaginative prayer and observe how deeply God touches those who open themselves up to God.

In fact the idea for this book came out of my (Jeannie's) unfruitful search for a resource on imaginative prayer. Larry regularly led imaginative prayer experiences for adults. I attended his sessions enough times to believe God could use imaginative prayer to touch students as well, but I couldn't find a resource. So we decided to write one.

This book is designed to help you invite others into God's presence through imaginative prayer. The bulk of the content is 50 exercises, written in easy-to-follow form. We've also included specific suggestions and ideas to enhance each prayer experience.

Through these exercises you and your students can open your imaginations to God's Spirit and allow God to move and speak directly to you. You'll be encouraged to hear God's words, see God's face, and experience God's touch in very personal ways. There are exercises that lead you through Bible stories and others that look at specific images of God. Some exercises are attached to church calendars and can be used to draw out deeper meanings from those dates during the year.

But please don't jump straight into the exercises before spending time in the beginning sections of this book. We offer all kinds of ideas and suggestions on how to lead students into imaginative prayer, to create emotionally safe experiences, as well as lists of suggested resources and props to enhance your physical settings.

We also include an important section on developmental and psychological issues. We want you to be aware of what may come up for your students when they allow God to touch their imaginations and emotions. Sometimes it's a pretty intense experience, and that can be confusing for teenagers—adults, too! We want to prepare you for that possibility and equip you to know how to respond wisely.

You'll even find information that offers solid credence for using imagination in spiritual formation. You may need that. People who haven't experienced imaginative prayer may have questions and concerns about it. We offer our thoughts on how to respond to the skeptics by explaining this prayer practice from a biblical, God-centered, historical foundation.

INTRO TWO: "WHAT IS IMAGINATIVE PRAYER? SPEAK SLOWLY, PLEASE."

The words *imagination* and *prayer* may seem like weird words to put together. Or maybe they're intriguing and you're curious about the possibilities. We believe imagination and prayer belong together and that imaginative prayer is a powerful tool that God can use to form us spiritually.

Okay, now we've got some "'splainin'" to do. *Imagination*, according to Webster's, is "the act or power of forming a mental image of something not present to the senses or never before wholly perceived in (physical) reality." Such as picturing an event from history or thinking through options before making a choice. Imagination, created by God, allows us to place ourselves in stories, think about the future, and even make sense of the present. Imagination helps us analyze what we observe. It's significantly connected to our five senses, our feelings, as well as our minds.

Prayer, on the other hand, is defined by Webster's as "the act of communicating with a deity." It's any way we connect with God, come into God's presence, hear from God, or speak to God.

Now let's put these two definitions together. *Imaginative prayer* is connecting with and hearing from God through mental images. One of the most common examples is placing yourself in a biblical narrative (this is what the majority of the exercises in this book help you to do). For instance, picture yourself in the boat with Jesus as the seas grow rough, as water spills over the sides and onto the deck. You are there. Notice what's going on…notice what you're feeling. What do you sense Jesus doing in the midst of the storm?

Imaginative prayer helps us experience the story and hear, see, and touch God in new ways. It helps us move from external head knowledge of God to an internalized, deeper knowing of God.

As you continue through this book, you'll find more information that gives credence for the use of imagination in spiritual formation. You'll find the words *imagination* and *prayer* fit together beautifully, with one enhancing the other. Notice how often imagination is encouraged in Scripture, how often Jesus teaches in story. There is metaphor and symbol throughout the sacred text, and it invites us to use our imaginations to encounter God. So go exploring for yourself. (It's one thing to read about imaginative prayer and quite another to experience it. Besides, experiencing imaginative prayer is a must before introducing others to it.)

INTRO THREE: "COMBINING THE WORDS *IMAGINATION* AND *PRAYER* MAKES ME NERVOUS. IT DOESN'T SOUND ENTIRELY CHRISTIAN."

You're not alone. In fact, we came from Christian traditions that would be very cautious—if not downright skeptical—of imaginative prayer. So we hear you. We both had to prayerfully figure out our own convictions about this prayer practice. You'll need to do the same. We encourage you to thoughtfully read the first section of this book, chapters 1 through 3, and pray for discernment of God's will for you and your ministry regarding this subject.

First, you'll hear our own stories—how God has used imaginative prayer to form us, heal us, and help us to see God and ourselves in newer, truer ways. You'll also read how blessed we've been to observe the transformational power of imaginative prayer in the lives of people we lead.

Then we'll break down how the Bible encourages imagination and how imaginative prayer has been used throughout church history. (It's not new, and it's not new age!) We'll go over some of the more common concerns about imaginative prayer and attempt to answer those concerns.

In worship God invites us to offer back to God all that's been created. And since God created imagination, we believe imaginative prayer is a beautiful, real-life example of following the command to "take captive every thought to make it obedient to Christ" (2 Corinthians 10:5b). With imaginative prayer, we give God control of our thoughts and imaginations, rather than trying to maintain control ourselves.

We know this can feel scary. Opening our thoughts, feelings, imaginations, and our very hearts before anyone—even God—can make us feel out of control. Jeannie can relate:

> *Each tiny step I take toward openness to God is still difficult for me—each inch feels scary, and sometimes I'm simply not ready to move.*

So it's okay if this isn't the right prayer practice for you or your ministry at this time.

However, we believe God invites each of us into more and more intimate knowledge of God and self. For us and for our ministries, we've found imaginative prayer a helpful and powerful part of our answer to that invitation. So we encourage you to consider whether or not it might also become part of your answer to God's invitation.

SECTION ONE
WHY?

CHAPTER 1

OUR STORIES

> IMAGINATION IS MORE IMPORTANT THAN KNOWLEDGE.
> FOR KNOWLEDGE IS LIMITED TO ALL WE *NOW* KNOW AND UNDERSTAND,
> WHILE IMAGINATION EMBRACES THE ENTIRE WORLD,
> AND ALL THERE EVER WILL BE TO KNOW AND UNDERSTAND.
> —*ALBERT EINSTEIN*

LARRY'S EXPERIENCE

When I became a Christian at age 17, I knew in my head that I was valued, loved, and accepted as I was; but it would take another 27 years to internalize this truth in my heart. In the fall of 2000 (now you know how old I am), the transforming power of imagination was made evident to me. I was attending a workshop called "Practicing the Presence of God" with 35 people I didn't know. We sat in a stark classroom behind uncomfortable school desks. I was one of only two men in attendance.

The workshop was progressing. Nothing new. I was thinking I could teach this rather easily. Then the leader said, "I'm going to play a movie, and I want you to imagine that the man is Jesus and the woman is you." Now for 33 of us, this would be pretty easy; but for me, and maybe for the other guy as well, this was a stretch. (I don't have the greatest imagination, believe it or not.) The good thing was that I'd watched this movie a half-dozen times. As the leader described the clips, I knew exactly what I would see. I could even recall major parts of the dialogue.

The lights went out, the familiar clips came on, and the tears streamed down my face. I heard sobs coming from deep within me. I was suddenly alone with Jesus, and he was speaking words of love, value, and delight straight into my heart. I embraced and held the movie's life-transforming, freedom-giving, hope-inspiring words as Jesus' words to *me*.

I entered the room that day as one who *knew* of God's love—I left that room as one who *personally experienced* God's love. My God-given, spirit-infused imagination allowed the truth and reality of God's wondrous love to span the infinite chasm of mind and heart for the first time, and I became richer and freer for it.

Afterward I was somewhat perplexed. In all my training and with all of my background experience, I'd never learned anything about the use of imagination. In fact, I typically would've resisted and been suspicious of someone promoting such a practice. But my experience was undeniable—not only that day, but as a transforming, spirit-shaping event.

Yet for a number of months, I still hesitated to share what happened to me. I did begin investigating the foundation for the use of imagination as a tool in spiritual formation. And what I discovered surprised me. The use of imagination was not something new and innovative, but it had been used in the church for centuries. This came to me not as an "Aha!" realization, but as a "Duh!" realization. All the images of the Bible flooded my mind—the parables of Jesus, the feasts of the Israelites, the bread and the cup. All of these encouraged—perhaps even *demanded*—the use of my imagination as a vehicle to embrace God and God's truth.

I began to use imagination as I spoke to groups of varying sizes and ages, and I did so in a number of different settings. In each instance God has used imaginative prayer to bring a deeper awareness of God's self and God's truth. I believe imaginative prayer helps create safe environments for people to bypass an overemphasis on their minds and freely open up their hearts to God.

Now when I enter situations that may tap into my sense of unworthiness or insecurity, I imagine God speaking words of love over me: "You are my beloved one, chosen, holy, uniquely valued in all the world; there is nothing that can ever separate you from my love, and there is nothing that can bring my condemnation upon you. I love you, and I am with you." These words empower me to go forward because not only are they God's words from the Bible, but they're also God's words to *me*.

Imaginative prayer brought to life God's love for me—and in a way that all my years of training during Bible college and seminary failed to do. My life, how I view myself, how I am with others, and how I do what I do have been forever changed.

JEANNIE'S EXPERIENCE

I entered middle school as an overweight, scared, lonely kid from a family struggling to find its way. We'd just moved from Orange County, California, to a Detroit suburb. I didn't have the right clothes or know the appropriate slang, and kids made fun of my accent. My imagination became a place of escape where I embraced my deepest desires to be known, loved, and worth rescuing. But when I left my imagination and returned to my reality, I was left feeling ugly, sad, and alone.

I sometimes wonder how my young teenage heart might have responded to imaginative prayer. What if I'd been encouraged to picture and experience God's smile of delight when God gazed at me? What might Jesus have whispered in my ear if I'd been encouraged to sit at his feet and listen? Perhaps I would have seen the truth of my beauty and value. Maybe I would have experienced God as my rescuer, lover, and friend, and viewed myself as beloved. And maybe those experiences would have helped heal my broken picture of myself.

Unfortunately, I never connected God with my imagination until about three years ago. While on a weeklong spiritual retreat, I was invited to live inside the biblical story of blind Bartimaeus:

> Then they came to Jericho. As Jesus and his disciples, together with a large crowd, were leaving the city, a blind man, Bartimaeus (that is, the Son of Timaeus), was sitting by the roadside begging. When he heard that it was Jesus of Nazareth, he began to shout, "Jesus, Son of David, have mercy on me!"
>
> Many rebuked him and told him to be quiet, but he shouted all the more, "Son of David, have mercy on me!" Jesus stopped and said, "Call him." So they called to the blind man, "Cheer up! On your feet! He's calling you." Throwing his cloak aside, he jumped to his feet and came to Jesus.
>
> "What do you want me to do for you?" Jesus asked him. The blind man said, "Rabbi, I want to see."
>
> "Go," said Jesus, "your faith has healed you." Immediately he received his sight and followed Jesus along the road. (Mark 10:46-52)

During the remainder of my retreat week, I thought a lot about Bartimaeus. I identified my own deep longing to call out to Jesus and my equally deep fear of being rebuked, rejected, or ignored. Then while I was considering the question Jesus posed, "What do you want me to do for you?" I was stunned. I always thought the goal was to figure out what Jesus wanted *me* to do and then dutifully obey. "What did *I* want?" I sat with that question for some time and wrote my answer the last day of the retreat: "Take me with you. Hold me close as your beloved child in whom you are well pleased."

Later I reread Mark 10:46-52. I considered how at the end of the passage, Jesus told Bartimaeus to go, but Bartimaeus chose to follow Jesus instead. Suddenly (and imaginatively) I was there. I was in Bartimaeus' place—a newly healed four-year-old child. The following is my journal entry:

> *I see myself following Jesus as a child. Holding his hand, skipping at his heels, nearly tripping him up, climbing onto his back...and then that's not enough, and he senses this. He pulls me around front. I say, "I want to stay with you, and I don't want you to ever leave me." He smiles, kisses my forehead, and says, "I won't ever leave you." I'm in his arms, tummy to tummy, with my legs wrapped around his back, and my arms around his neck. I lay my head on his shoulder and snuggle my face into his neck. I pull my head back up and look straight into his face. I ask, "Do you promise you won't leave?" He answers, "I promise I won't leave." I almost lay my head back down, but raise it again and ask, "Do you really, really promise?" He smiles so gently and lovingly. His eyes hold mine as he answers, "I really, really promise." I lay my head back down. I kiss his neck and snuggle in. I fall asleep as we travel.*

I had known in my head that God would never leave me, but apparently I hadn't *experienced* that truth. My imaginative prayer took my sense of knowing to a deeper level where I could begin to possess it as my own personal word from God. The picture of Jesus holding my four-year-old body while we journey together is a powerful image that continues to speak peace and courage into my spirit.

Through imaginative prayer God is rewriting some of the old, unhealthy images I've had of myself and of God. When I picture myself as the one sitting at Jesus' feet, I can feel Jesus' delight in me. I sense his gentleness and compassion for me in the midst of my weaknesses, fears, and sadness. Feeling fully known, accepted, and loved has freed me to begin letting go of my fears of failure and rejection and just "be" with the one who loves me most. Out of this place of savoring myself as Jesus' beloved, I see myself, God, and the world around me with new eyes. These eyes tend to live with more hope than fear nowadays, and as they look right back in the eyes of God, they seem to trustingly ask, "What's next, Papa?" (Romans 8:15, MSG).

I've led small groups of middle school girls for nearly 20 years. I think one of the reasons I'm drawn to this age group is because my middle school years were so difficult. Through their eyes I watch as the little girl disappears and the woman is born. It's a fragile time, and a time when I want to emphasize their belovedness above all else. I became convinced that imaginative prayer would be a wonderful way for these girls to more fully know their value and beauty to God. So I began to introduce imaginative prayer in those groups. It's been amazing to see how God meets them right where they are and gives them just what they're ready to hear.

CHAPTER 2

BEGINNINGS

THE CHRISTIAN IMAGINATION PLAYS A GREAT ROLE
IN THE SPIRITUAL DEVELOPMENT OF THE SOUL.

—ST. JOHN OF THE CROSS

Imagination is often dismissed as childish, a waste of time, worthless, or even evil. Yet we use our imaginations every day. Imagination is part of our daily planning, decision-making, and discernment processes. It's through imagination that we decide what to buy or eat, where to go on vacation, how to plan birthday parties, what classes to take in school, how to invite someone to the prom, or how to write a paper. Our imaginations give us the ability to dream, hope, learn from our pasts, and apply those discoveries to the present and future. They help us move ahead in big and small ways. We all use our imaginations. It's how we live life.

Again, according to Webster's, *imagination* is "the act or power of forming a mental image of something not present to the senses or never before wholly perceived in (physical) reality." Such as "seeing" the face of a child as she opens the gift you're planning to give her or picturing yourself in the career you've chosen to pursue.

As we discuss imagination throughout this book, we would add an additional component to the definition. It's what C. S. Lewis calls "baptized" imagination, or what Bruce Demarest refers to as the "sanctified" use of imagination. In other words, using imagination in a God-focused way, functioning within the framework of God's revealed character and truth. It's using imagination as guided and directed by the Spirit of God and informed by the living Word of God. As we intentionally use our imaginations in this way, it gives us the ability to experientially enter into the stories, symbolism, and images of the Bible.

It empowers us to hold the present with both the past and future and to see and embrace the seen (physical) and the unseen (eternal). The Spirit-infused imagination moves us from sterile head knowledge to life-transforming, heart-healing, biblically informed ways of being and doing life. It's as we embrace and employ the use of our God-given, Spirit-infused imaginations that we can enter the wonder and mystery of God and God's Word.

The use of imagination plays a critical role in the holistic spiritual development of Christians. This has always been true. In the next few pages, we'll introduce you to voices from the past and present that affirm the importance and benefits of imagination for spiritual formation. In addition, we hope you'll be excited to discover the greatest literary work that we believe affirms and even demands the use of imagination—the Bible.

SCRIPTURE

The opening words of the Bible, "In the beginning," could easily have been, "Once upon a time." The Bible is story. It encourages us—even incites us—to enter its pages in imaginative ways.

In the opening chapters of Genesis, the earth is formless and void, and the Spirit of God moves across its surface. Sunlight, sky, mountains, valleys, and all of life are created through God's imagination. The final book of the Bible, Revelation, bursts with dramatic images and descriptions of Jesus, heaven, the turmoil of the world, and the birth of a new heaven and earth. The whole of Scripture demands our fully engaged imaginations to enter into and embrace this amazing story of creation and redemption, of good versus evil, of power, love, grace, and hope.

The Bible is filled with imagery and metaphor. We find God portrayed as rock, eagle, mother, and father (Deuteronomy 32:4, 11, 18). Jesus is referred to as the Bread of Life (John 6:35), the True Vine (John 15:1), and the Lamb (John 1:29). The Holy Spirit is pictured as a dove (Matthew 3:16), as fire (Acts 2:3), and as streams of living water (John 7:38-39). Jesus speaks of the kingdom of heaven as a mustard seed (Matthew 13:31) and a treasure hidden in a field (Matthew 13:44). The church is imaged as a body (1 Corinthians 12:12-27), bride (Revelation 19:7), and flock (Acts 20:28).

The Bible is written imaginatively because we're imaginative. These dramatic pictures exist to help us enter into the living Word of God, to gaze upon the Lord (Psalm 27:4), to look beyond the seen to the unseen (2 Corinthians 4:18), and to fully embrace the truth that in God we live, move, and have our being (Acts 17:28).

Imagination gives us wings to soar into the wonder, mystery, and truth of God and God's Word.

SYMBOLS

Historically Christians and churches have drawn upon symbols to express the wonder and mystery of the Christian faith. Many of us pay special attention to the cross and crucifix, bread and wine, baptism, oil, and light, but the list can also include anything from church-sanctioned icons to sunsets or an empty seat at the table. Each symbol calls us to do more than cognitively understand it. They invite us to employ our imaginations and explore the depths of the symbols, experiencing the meaning and transforming power resulting from our interaction with the truth they represent.

WISDOM FROM THE PAST

Using imagination within the church is not a recent invention. Throughout church history people have used their imaginations and taught others to do the same to help experience and internalize the life-healing, soul-enriching, hope-sustaining truths of God. Those associated with the use of imagination include Saint Gregory of Nyssa, Origen of Alexandria, St. Augustine, St. Teresa of Avila, St. John of the Cross, St. Ignatius of Loyola, St. Francis de Sales, and Julian of Norwich.

But the figure who most significantly elevated the use of imagination was St. Ignatius of Loyola. This isn't surprising, since it was Ignatius' imagination that introduced him to Jesus Christ in a spiritually transforming way. The turning point in his life came after a cannonball broke his leg during a battle (that'll leave a mark). Throughout the long hours of recovery, he spent time imagining his future exploits as a soldier (once he was fully recovered), as well as reading a book about the lives of the saints. Initially Ignatius' imagined military exploits excited him, but they were quickly replaced with feelings of restlessness and dissatisfaction. Then one day he imagined what it would be like to live as the saints in that book. As he did this, he noticed feelings of excitement and transformation in his heart and soul, leaving him at peace and satisfied. God used Ignatius' imagination to transform him into a follower of Christ.

In his writings, especially *Spiritual Exercises*, Ignatius instructs readers to imaginatively enter the gospel story; to see, smell, taste, touch, and hear what's unfolding around them. He saw imagination as the place where we can experience, embrace, and internalize spiritual truth. So we don't merely *read* about the manger, the garden, and the cross—we're present to hear the cries of the newborn King, to feel a son's pain as he pleads with his father and struggles within himself, and to see the nails driven into the tender flesh of our Savior.

For Ignatius, imagination unites past with present and brings us face-to-face with the living God. For him, the use of imagination is essential to prayer and transformation.

WISDOM FROM THE PRESENT

The use of imagination for spiritual understanding is still alive and well. Richard Foster, author of numerous books on spiritual formation, including *Celebration of Discipline*, discusses the benefits of using our imaginations when we interact with Scripture. In his book *Prayer: Finding the Heart's True Home*, he writes:

> We begin to enter the story and make it our own. We move from detached observation to active participation. Using the imagination also brings the emotions into the equation so that we can come to God with both mind and heart.

Oswald Chambers, author of *My Utmost for His Highest*, warns against neglecting our imaginations:

> The starvation of the imagination is one of the most fruitful sources of exhaustion and sapping in a worker's life. If you have never used your imagination to put yourself before God, begin to do it now...Imagination is the greatest gift God has given us, and it ought to be devoted to Him.

In his book *Preaching & Teaching with Imagination: The Quest for Biblical Ministry*, popular biblical commentator Warren Wiersbe echoes Chambers' opinion:

> Christians who ignore or neglect the cultivating of their imagination can't enter into the full enjoyment of all that God has for them. A sanctified imagination opens the door to so much that is beautiful and enriching that it's a pity more believers don't realize what they are missing and do something about it.

And Eugene Peterson, author of *The Message*, writes in *Under the Unpredictable Plant*:

> For Christians whose largest investment is in the invisible [eternal], the imagination is indispensable...Right now one of the essential Christian ministries in our ruined world is the recovery and exercise of the imagination...imagination is the mental tool we have for connecting material and spiritual,

visible and invisible, earth and heaven…imagination catapults us into mystery.

These theological thinkers and writers take us back to the Bible itself. And it's the Bible—with its use of imagery, symbolism, poetry, parable, and narrative—that argues most strongly for using imagination. And it is God, the Author of the Bible, who not only encourages and incites the use of imagination, but also sanctifies and baptizes it. God invites us to sacrificially offer our imaginations to God and to receive the healing and transformation that come from encountering our loving and gracious God.

CHAPTER 3

CONCERNS AND RESPONSES

> TO BELIEVE THAT GOD CAN SANCTIFY
> AND UTILIZE THE IMAGINATION IS
> SIMPLY TO TAKE SERIOUSLY THE
> CHRISTIAN IDEA OF INCARNATION.
>
> — *RICHARD FOSTER*

Does the idea of using imagination in a spiritual context freak you out? Or are you concerned it might freak out some parents or church leaders? It might. We want to help you approach imaginative prayer with enthusiasm and confidence, so we've listed some of the common questions and responded to them.

Aren't we opening ourselves up to being deceived when we use our imaginations? We're not opening ourselves up to darkness and deception, but to receive God's light and truth. It's important to look at the fruit that's produced through using our imaginations. Does it lead us closer to or further away from God? Does it lead toward or away from peace, joy, passion for others, and knowledge of self? The Spirit-led imagination helps us stop controlling what we think we know and starts letting God guide our heads and hearts. We're admitting that our thoughts aren't God's thoughts (Isaiah 55:8) and placing our trust squarely in the lap of God, inviting God to give us understanding and guidance (Proverbs 3:5-6). The imagination that's given by God is dramatically obedient to 2 Corinthians 10:5, where we're told to "take captive every thought to make it obedient to Christ." We're inviting God to show us our blind spots—to show us where we've been deceived.

That said, if our imaginations aren't Spirit-led, they can lie to us. If a student comes out of imaginative prayer with a "message from God" that seems outside the character of God, you may need to explore it sensitively with that student. It's an opportunity to walk with that student into a deeper understanding of who God is and what God's about. We have a sidebar that specifically deals with this issue—"You Heard God Say What?" (see page 47).

Isn't objective or absolute truth minimized by imagination? We believe God is absolute and objective Truth. We also believe that God speaks through Scripture, people, creation, art, and within our own hearts and imaginations to show us this Truth. But we see "through a glass darkly" (1 Corinthians 13:12)—through our own limited, subjective lens. Since God (Truth) honors our desire to know God and ourselves more fully, we can experience peace that our imaginative prayers will help lead us to God.

Since other religions and spirituality streams use imaginative meditation, how can it be Christian? The use of imagination has been associated with Christianity from the earliest times. (See chapter 2, page 21, for more on that.) The fact that non-Christians have discovered the power of the imagination doesn't nullify its use in our case. Rather than running from the God-given gift of imagination just because others have adopted it, we suggest reclaiming it for the holy use God intended.

Doesn't imagination deal with fantasy? If we're called to teach truth and reality, how does using our imaginations fit into that? Truth and reality aren't strangers to imagination; they're companions. Jesus taught deep truths using images, metaphors, and symbols. Imagination can reinforce truth or lies. Since choosing to avoid imagination isn't an option, we must instead choose to allow God to guide our imaginations toward truth. God offers us true, Spirit-led images of ourselves and of God that bring freedom and life.

Since the Bible says, "The heart is deceitful above all things and beyond cure. Who can understand it?" (Jeremiah 17:9) how can we trust our imaginations? We aren't asking you to trust *your* imagination, but to trust in God's transforming power and vested interest in making God more deeply and truly known and experienced. We're inviting you to trust the Holy Spirit to lead and guide you into truth. You're not alone in this—God is with you, God's Spirit is within you, and God's Word offers boundaries for the use of your imagination. We're encouraging you to trust the God who has given you a new heart and the mind of Christ—the God who has sanctified your imagination.

Doesn't the second commandment, "You shall not make for yourself an idol...you shall not bow down to them or worship them" (Exodus 20:4-5), rule out the use of imagination? This commandment prohibits the use of physical creation as objects of worship. It isn't prohibiting the use of imagination. The Bible itself uses a variety of images to picture God; and again, Jesus' own words are filled with imagery (see chapter 1).

Isn't it idolatrous and heretical to picture the infinite and invisible God in a finite way? Throughout the Bible are a number of finite pictures that communicate something of who God is. In other words, they're incomplete. But like it or not, we all have pictures of God in our minds. And the good news is that as we enter into, interact with, and ponder images of God, our perceptions of and interactions with God can be expanded, replacing more limited images with truer, personal, healing, and transforming images of God.

SECTION TWO
HOW?

CHAPTER 4

ANY TAKERS?

USING THE IMAGINATION ALSO BRINGS THE EMOTIONS
INTO THE EQUATION, SO THAT WE COME TO GOD WITH
BOTH MIND AND HEART. IT IS VITALLY IMPORTANT TO UNDERSTAND
THE SCRIPTURE INTELLECTUALLY, BUT IF WE HAVE NOT
FELT IT EMOTIONALLY, WE HAVE NOT FULLY UNDERSTOOD IT.

— *RICHARD FOSTER*

ARE YOU READY FOR THIS?

Answer the following questions:

1. Do you want to see, hear, and taste that the Lord is good?

2. Does the idea of Jesus looking into your eyes and whispering personal words into your ear sound a bit like heaven?

3. Do you believe you're held safely in God's loving hand and that God honors your desire to know and experience God?

4. Are you excited about the idea of using your imagination in prayer?

5. Do you believe God greatly desires for you to personally *experience* God, rather than simply know about God?

If you answered "yes" to any of these questions, then you're a great candidate for being powerfully transformed through imaginative prayer, and we're excited that this book is in your hands. But before you consider whether or not to use guided meditations with your students, it's important that you experience imaginative prayer for yourself.

We invite you to pick a few exercises from this book (they begin on page 52) and allow yourself to imaginatively enter into the stories. It's usually easier to free your imagination when you don't have to read the story yourself, so we suggest you find a comfy spot and ask a friend to read a meditation to you. (It's also effective to record your reading of the meditation and then play it back while you imaginatively enter the story.)

Get into a relaxed, comfortable position. Take a couple of deep, slow breaths, internally quieting down. Ask God to prepare your heart and to guide and direct your prayer. As the meditation is read slowly, gently enter and become part of the scene. As you participate in imaginative prayer, notice what God's invitation is for you. What do you hear, see, feel, or sense? What is being given to you in this moment?

When you sense that the time of imaginative prayer is ending, take a few additional minutes to sit with your experience in prayerful silence. You may wish to conclude your time with a prayer of thanksgiving, commitment, or confession. Journaling may be helpful as well. End your prayer in whatever way seems to naturally flow out of your experience.

Afterward consider these questions:

- What was your comfort level?

- What made the experience easy or hard?

- What could be added or removed that might have deepened your experience of God?

Take notes on what you discover so you can use these insights if you decide to lead others in imaginative prayer.

ARE YOUR STUDENTS READY FOR THIS?

If you've experienced God in deeper ways through imaginative prayer, that's great! We hope you'll continue to offer your imagination to God and trust God to use it in life-transforming ways. But now it's decision time. *Would this practice be helpful to students? Is now the time to introduce students to imaginative prayer? If so, how will I do that?*

If God is nudging you toward imaginative prayer, there are some things to think about. There are many ways to lead imaginative prayer: You can guide students through meditations in large groups, small groups, or individually. You can split the girls from the guys or keep them together. You can use it with just your student leaders. There are also many ways to customize an imaginative prayer experience. The next two chapters go into detail regarding these and other issues.

COUNT THE COST

As you move toward using imaginative prayer with your group, consider your church culture and ministry situation. If you think you'll be met with resistance, be especially careful to lay a good foundation with your supervisor and the other adults associated with your ministry. It's important that they support and understand your use of imaginative prayer. These folks can be lifesavers as you deal with conflict, and they can create a smooth pathway for you to follow your heart and God's leading for imaginative prayer in your ministry.

People may come to you expressing concern, resistance, or even contempt for the use of imagination. It's important to understand where they're coming from. People tend to resist for one of three reasons:

1. **They don't understand what you're doing.** They come to you confused but with openness and a desire to understand. Share your heart with them, talk about the value imagination plays throughout the Bible and church history, and describe the many benefits it can bring to your students.

2. **They don't like it.** When reaction is strong, try to quickly determine if they're willing to dialogue. They may have big concerns because of their backgrounds or their perspectives on certain Bible passages. Yet they may honestly wish to hear you and be heard by you. On the other hand, they may be angry or hostile. If so, beware. It's best to make it a quick conversation. Listen politely and then refer them to your supervisor.

3. **They don't like you.** They've been waiting for the opportunity to pounce—and here it is. They're not willing to hear and they don't want to understand. Therefore, listen politely while resisting the temptation to strike back. Again, refer them to your supervisor.

ANY TAKERS?

Still interested? Are you excited to move on and jump right into the exercises with your students? Wait! Don't skip to the back and find the exercises just yet. Consider "wasting" a bit more time in this section of the book. We want to share with you some foundational "how-to" information in chapters 5 and 6 that could be really helpful.

THE TIMING COULDN'T BE BETTER
—MARV PENNER (AUTHOR, SPEAKER, YOUTH MINISTRY PROFESSOR)

Recent research shows that the teenage brain goes through some major changes in early and mid-adolescence. Along with puberty comes a gradual but significant increase in the number of brain cells (neurons) the body produces. At the same time, the connections between those cells (synapses) also become more efficient. Scientists believe this increased efficiency, along with opportunities to practice creative and conceptual thinking (imagination), will allow teenagers to start processing information more abstractly and use their minds more productively.

But here's the problem. According to the research of Dr. Jay Giedd at the National Institute of Mental Health in Bethesda, Maryland: If you don't use it, you lose it. He explains that a few years after this peak in neuron and synapse development, the brain begins to shrink in size and only those connections that have been used and developed will remain.

What does this mean for us as we guide teenagers toward the use of imaginative prayer? There may be a window of opportunity during kids' peak periods of brain development in which they can use their God-given imaginations in their prayer lives. And teenagers who can imaginatively see how their stories are deeply connected to God's story will have a more tangible sense of God's presence. Most importantly, kids who learn to pray with the full range of God-given creativity and imagination will establish patterns that will stay with them into adulthood.

The teenage transition to abstract thinking takes place over time and won't be experienced at the same pace by every adolescent in your care. Since early adolescents may not be as equipped (in terms of cognitive development) as those who are a bit older and better able to think conceptually, they may not be able to participate fully in these exercises.

Also, some kids have life circumstances (trauma, lack of cognitive stimulation, learning disabilities, and so on) that may make it more challenging for them to fully engage in the prayer exercises in this book. Be patient with them. Adapt the task to make it more accessible if you can, coach them as they try new ways of praying, and recognize that your investment will pay big dividends both now and in the future.

CHAPTER 5

DEVELOPING THE ENVIRONMENT

ONLY IN MEN'S IMAGINATION DOES EVERY TRUTH FIND
AN EFFECTIVE AND UNDENIABLE EXISTENCE. IMAGINATION,
NOT INVENTION, IS THE SUPREME MASTER OF ART AS OF LIFE.

—JOSEPH CONRAD (1857-1924), POLISH-BORN BRITISH NOVELIST

Before beginning an overview of the externals, we want to reintroduce the role you'll play in all of this. Mark Yaconelli, in his book *Contemplative Youth Ministry*, writes, "A note of caution, it can be incredibly painful, even destructive for kids to be led in…a spiritual exercise by people who have little experience" (195, Youth Specialties/Zondervan, 2006). It's important that you've experienced imaginative prayer for yourself—not only once, but a number of times—and that you've found it a helpful and meaningful way to connect with and hear from God. This is the foundation for creating a healthy and positive environment for your students.

Once that foundation exists and you sense comfort and excitement with imaginative prayer, we invite you to consider the environment you'd like to create for your students. This environment can either help or hinder the depth and richness of imaginative prayer. We encourage you to set aside some time to think through how you can create an environment that—

- Communicates safety, grace, and love

- Helps free your students from distractions

- Helps focus your students' hearts and minds

- Reinforces the subject or setting of the exercise

COMMUNICATE SAFETY, GRACE, AND LOVE

As your students are invited into imaginative prayer, it's critical that they feel as though they're entering a safe and caring environment. You're not looking for "right answers" or "right responses." Instead, you're inviting them to be with God in whatever way God chooses. This is only possible when you and your staff let God be God and trust that God will hold the hearts of your students gently. You may want to pause a moment and search your own heart. Do you have an agenda for what your students will take away from their experiences? Can you hold loosely to your hopes and allow God to set the agenda?

PHYSICAL ENVIRONMENT

Once you've settled on an exercise, prayerfully read through it a couple of times while asking yourself and God, *What type of environment would help this exercise come alive, yet would also help my students focus and not become distracted?* As you slowly read through the exercise, a number of ideas, thoughts, or vague senses of what you might do may begin to emerge. Write these down and slowly read through it again.

LOCATION

The exercise may involve water, so the idea of either sitting around a fountain or going to a pool, lake, or even the ocean might float through your mind. Write it all down; then return to your ideas and think through the pros and cons of each one.

- **Identify potential distractions.** Can people wander through uninvited? Is weather a potential hazard? What about lighting? Noise? You're trying to create an environment that encourages and supports quiet reflection. Loudly ticking clocks, sound checks next door, lawn mowers, or scorching temperatures usually aren't helpful. Can the distractions be removed or avoided? It's best to find a location where you have a good amount of control over what people see, hear, and feel within your environment.

- **How much can you change up the setting?** Can you move things around, hang things from the ceiling, use candles, bring food? How much freedom do you have to transform this place into something very different? This transformation process powerfully enhances the experience of imaginative prayer. This is especially true when you transform a familiar place like the youth room, sanctuary, or gym into a space with a whole different look and feel.

Consider the pros and cons of your location choices, but don't be afraid to experiment. It's a learning process. You'll probably need to lead your students through an imaginative prayer exercise or two before you can know for sure how easily distracted they will be and how carefully you'll need to monitor outside distractions. And you probably won't fully understand what a particular location has to offer until you actually use it.

Once you've chosen your exercise and your location (removing whatever distractions you can), then it's time to consider what you can do to transform the setting into a magical space—a portal into the presence of God. (Okay, maybe that's a tad unrealistic, but ask yourself, *What can I do—given the available time, energy, and resources—to help enhance my students' experiences?*)

In youth ministry we often encourage the use of high-energy sights and sounds. They may catch people's attention, but oftentimes they're not very helpful in developing imaginative prayer environments. So instead we'd like to encourage you to help your students see, hear, feel, taste, smell, and fully experience whatever God is offering them by engaging their senses in thoughtful and purposeful ways. It will help them to use their imaginations, connect with their emotions, and deepen their prayer experiences.

ENGAGING THE FIVE SENSES

SIGHT

Look around. What about your setting encourages students to see God? How can that be enhanced? The tone of the room is greatly impacted by lighting and color. A few candles can make a huge difference over fluorescent lights! Colorful blankets, pillows, or draped fabric can soften the look of a normally sterile room.

Use art. Consider photographs, paintings, or sculptures. Bring visuals of Christ, the cross or crucifix, nature, faces of people, piles of trash, pictures of despair and hope. Place these around the room or in a central location by creating an altar.

Use media. Art can be presented on a screen, as well as being physically displayed in a setting. Words can also be projected to help create this space of prayer. Show video clips of storms, deserts, or sunrises. These can help your students enter into the narrative more fully.

SOUND

Ambient music can work wonders. You may want to post a sign on the outside door asking people to turn off their cell phones and enter the room quietly.

We all know different music evokes different moods and emotions. You can find or create CDs with sounds of nature. These can be gentle and peaceful or turbulent and stormy. There can be birds singing or wolves howling, the sounds of laughter or crying, people singing or yelling.

The voice of the person reading the meditation is a big part of developing the environment for prayer. Consider the tone of your voice and the pace of your reading. Decide whether it's best to use your voice simply, so you don't distract from the words, or dramatically, to enhance the words of the meditation.

SMELL

Smell can calm, excite, or repulse. Smells can also bring to mind past events and create new memories. Scented candles or incense are easy to get and can create a calming environment.

You can either bring new smells to your usual setting or take your students to alternate settings with specific smells. Be creative and experiment. Consider where you'll encounter fragrant flowers, eucalyptus, or pine trees. Walk through the woods. Sit in a barn. Go where you can smell the ocean. Lead your meditation next to a smelly dumpster and imaginatively enter the story of a homeless beggar.

A word of caution: Engaging the sense of smell can also prove horribly distracting. People have allergies and some have weak stomachs. Be wise!

TASTE

Include something salty, bitter, or sweet to enhance an imaginative prayer experience. Have your students eat a meal in silence and truly taste each bite. Have them notice the varieties of flavor, texture, and temperature that God has created for their enjoyment and nourishment. Have them eat bread as they consider that Jesus is the Bread of Life. Give them water to drink as they sit with the reality of Jesus as the living water and their source of life.

TOUCH

The sense of touch is highly underutilized. Especially for your more tactile kids, having an object to touch can actually help free their minds and imaginations. Throw pillows and blankets are easy to add to a room, and they tend to encourage physical and emotional relaxation. Allow them to cuddle up with silk or fleece or burlap. Use clay. Ask them to pour water, hammer nails, or lay their hands on the rough wood of a cross.

PUTTING IT ALL TOGETHER

Consider your imaginative prayer exercise, the limitations and opportunities in your chosen location, and your available resources for enhancing the physical space. As you begin the process of transformation, it's helpful to have support from people who enjoy creative thinking and design. If you choose to make imaginative prayer an ongoing part of your ministry, it might be helpful to create a traveling storage system for your supplies. For more information, see "The Imaginative Prayer Treasure Chest" sidebar on page 37.

A WORD OF CAUTION

Though the physical environment is important, it's not the crucial piece of the equation. Here's how Larry remembers leading an imaginative prayer experience with people of all ages and from a variety of denominational backgrounds:

> *They didn't know me, and most of them had never experienced imaginative prayer before. Added to this mix was a worship band going through a series of sound checks in a room below us. Although I tried to get the worship band to sound check another time, it didn't work out. For the next three mornings, in the midst of our quiet and serene environment, we were bombarded by jagged drum, bass, and guitar sounds. Yet, in spite of it all, it turned into a very powerful experience. Many tears were shed, and afterward people expressed a deeper sense of God's love.*

We've led imaginative prayer exercises in a variety of environments, and we've found that the most important thing is not the setting, but *you*. Are you prayerfully entering this experience yourself? Are you comfortable with imaginative prayer? And are you able—by your presence and words—to create an environment in which students feel safe and free to enter this experience, not feeling coerced or sensing hidden agendas or unspoken expectations? Do they find themselves in a place of love, acceptance, and grace?

You'll need to walk the tricky path of creating a setting that fosters and enhances your students' experiences without manipulating them toward a "correct" discovery. So we suggest being mindful of the fine line between enhancement and manipulation, between opening space for God to speak and speaking for God.

THE IMAGINATIVE PRAYER TREASURE CHEST

The term *treasure chest* refers to that jewel-encrusted container, cardboard box, big plastic bag, or whatever you decide will best hold the precious resources you beg, borrow, buy, or steal (we neither endorse nor condone thievery) to enhance imaginative prayer experiences.

The idea is simple: Gather and store your supplies in containers that are easy to get your hands on whenever needed.

BENEFITS OF AN IMAGINATIVE PRAYER TREASURE CHEST

- It dramatically increases the likelihood that you'll spend time enhancing the environment.

- It reduces stress, the amount of time needed, and the potential expense involved in enhancing the environment.

- It helps you to get others involved. Point them to the chest, and let them go at it.

- It gives you freedom to do creative, impromptu worship and prayer experiences as well.

STARTER TREASURE CHEST

So what kinds of trinkets should go into your starter treasure chest? Here are some simple ideas to consider:

- Candles. The ones that come in glass jars work great and tend to be safer and cleaner than other candles.

- Lighter and matches. Have both. Your lighter will eventually run out of fuel.

- A cross or crucifix. A freestanding one works well. (Larry has a four-foot wooden cross that works great, but it's heavy and bulky to lug around.)

- Art and writing supplies. Include various colors, types, and sizes of paper and a variety of writing utensils: pens, pencils, colored pencils, markers, and crayons. (Note: Don't try to save money on crayons—all crayons are *not* created equal.) Also have scissors, tape, glue sticks, and stickers. Storing these supplies in plastic bags or inexpensive plastic containers helps keep the items in good shape.

- Music. Include nature sounds or ambient music; movie soundtracks often include good instrumental numbers. Don't forget to include the necessary device for playing the music! Larry has an iPod with a portable speaker system. Thus, he says, "I can have all the music I'd ever want available all the time—but I do *not* keep it in the treasure chest."

- Fabric table coverings. Fabric softens the feel of a room. You can drape fabric around a cross or altar and use fabric-covered tables for debriefing times.

- Blankets. Mexican blankets work well. They're colorful, usually cheap (at least they are if you live near the border of Mexico), and good to sit or lie down on when outside. They also add coziness to sterile rooms.

THE LIST GOES ON

Here are some more supplies to consider adding along the way. But you must also consider your own personality and setting. And consider your budget, too!

- Stamps and inkpads. These are pricey, so collect them slowly. They're great for making cards. A debriefing idea might be to make a card for Jesus expressing your experience with him during the exercise. When you finish your card, imagine yourself giving it to Jesus.

- Clay. Multicolored clay is fun. Students can use it to communicate a truth, insight, or awareness they received during the prayer time.

- Finger paints. You may also want to include newsprint and rags. Using color and motion, students can capture and communicate their prayer experiences.

- Watercolors. Buy the watercolors that come in tubes and use paper plates as palettes. Use paper cups for the water. Also, watercolor paper is helpful. Cheap brushes work fine.

- Communion cup and plate. Communion taken individually or as a group with one person serving another can be a powerful way to end imaginative prayer.

- Magazines. These can be used to create photographic collages. Be careful with your choice of magazines, since some can be more distracting than helpful.

- Craft scissors, Popsicle sticks, pipe cleaners. Nice additions to the art supplies.

- Bells or chimes. They can call students back together, end a time of silence, or indicate a transition when the use of a voice might be a distraction.

- Baskets or gallon-sized, plastic storage bags with zipper tops. May be useful to keep various supplies intact or separated.

- Bubble machine. Very cool.

- Small, portable fountain. The sound of running water can really enhance certain imaginative exercises.

- Portable lights. Spotlights with different colored bulbs can be used to create different moods.

- Ocean drum. It makes crashing wave sounds.

- Fog machine. This could really create a nice feel, but consider good ventilation and kids with asthma.

- Rocks. They're so handy, and they can be used as symbols for so many things. Black ones can be used in combination with a white pen. Write words on the rock as a way to debrief.

- Febreze Scentstories. A small machine that uses scent-themed discs to add fragrance to a room. See www.scentstories.com.

This list isn't exhaustive. In fact, it doesn't contain all of the things Larry has in his Treasure Chest—one side of his garage is stacked from floor to ceiling with stuff! But hopefully this gives you some ideas for items you can use and different ways to make use of them.

Now, it's not necessary to buy all this stuff at once (although having your own bubble machine is quite cool). Start by gathering some basic items and then build slowly from there, if you need to. You may even want to create a "wish list" to pass out to your youth group students and parents. You never know what people will be willing to donate!

CHAPTER 6

THE BASICS

> I AM A RATIONALIST. FOR ME, REASON IS THE
> NATURAL ORGAN OF TRUTH; BUT IMAGINATION IS THE
> ORGAN OF MEANING. IMAGINATION...
> IS NOT THE CAUSE OF TRUTH, BUT ITS CONDITION.
>
> *—C.S. LEWIS*

The imaginative prayer exercises in this book are designed to help your students enter into story and come face-to-face with God—to hear God's words and experience God's love. But this won't happen automatically. For you to increase the likelihood of imaginative prayer being a positive and powerfully transforming experience for your students, there are a couple of things you can do.

PRAY

For yourself, your students, the experience, and the time following the exercise—pray. Be open to new ideas and the gentle prompting of God's Spirit. A prayerful awareness of God's presence will help you discern God's leading as you facilitate the imaginative prayer experience.

EXPLAIN

Tell your students what to expect. This is always wise, even if your group is familiar with imaginative prayer. There may be new people in your group; but even if there aren't, a reminder is helpful. This way everyone will begin on the same page.

Here are some thoughts on what might be helpful to share with your students:

- **What it is.** Imaginative prayer is a way of opening ourselves to God and listening for God's words, looking for God's face, and waiting for God's touch. It's a way of praying that can help us experience God's truth in life-changing ways.

- **What it isn't.** It's not magic. Imaginative prayer doesn't cause God to show up. God is always here and always with us—imaginative prayer simply helps us open ourselves to experience that.

- **Don't force it.** Gently enter into imaginative prayer by asking God to guide and direct you. Regardless of whether or not you "feel" anything, you offered yourself to God as a gift—an act that is pleasing and honoring to God.

- **It might feel a little weird**. This may be a new way to pray. It may feel a little weird and uncomfortable at first, but I encourage you to give it a try. I've found—*(briefly share your experience, including initial feelings of uncertainty, discomfort, excitement, and how you feel about it now)*. Do what you can, and trust that God will meet you where you are.

WE'RE ALL DIFFERENT

Because people have different levels of ability when it comes to imagining, it's good to name that and briefly talk about those differences. (See sidebar on page 42, "But I Don't Have a Good Imagination!")

SOME GUIDELINES

These guidelines are important to communicate to your students. This is especially true for those with little biblical background and little or no understanding of God or Scripture. The use of imaginative prayer isn't an open-ended free-for-all. We're suggesting time-tested guidelines that can give shape and form to the experience and help people stay focused on God and God's words to them.

- Place yourself in the story as a specific character or onlooker or as instructed by your leader. Once in the story, be open to letting God change your role. If this happens, notice who you are, your age, your part of the story.

- Allow yourself to sink into the setting. What do you see and feel, taste, touch, smell? What is being said? To whom is it said? Are words addressed to you?

- Be aware if you're drawn to something or resistant to doing something or going somewhere. Just notice this and continue to involve yourself in the story, allowing it to unfold around you.

- Gently seek to make contact with God…eye contact, a face-to-face encounter, a dialogue, a sitting with…pay attention to your feelings, any words spoken by God to you.

- Remember to evaluate all that happens in your imagination in light of the character and Word of God. Put aside any images that are in opposition to God's character and Scripture.

- Resist the temptation to interpret what's happening. Instead *be a part* of what's happening.

BUT I DON'T HAVE A GOOD IMAGINATION!

Everyone has an imagination, but some are underdeveloped and stifled by a culture that tends to view imagination as an activity for children or a common practice of irresponsible daydreamers. So as you encourage the use of imagination, be aware that you and your students may sense inadequacy or internal resistance.

In addition, we usually think of imagination in terms of watching movies in our minds—something visual. But many people don't imagine this way at all! Some imagine through their sense of hearing—they hear the sounds associated with the scene, like the roar of a crowd or the ripple of a brook. Others imagine through emotion—they feel what's going on, sensing anger or joy within a story—and they experience those emotions themselves. Others instinctively know what's happening in a narrative and can even describe it, but they may not initially see, hear, or feel what's taking place.

The point is that there are various ways to imagine. Encourage your students to imagine as they can, not as they can't. However their imagination works—through seeing, hearing, feeling, or some combination of these three—the important thing is that they feel free to begin where they are and are assured that God will meet them there.

WHEN IT HURTS TO GO DEEP...

For some of your students, the opportunity to venture into the world of imaginative prayer may feel frightening and maybe even dangerous. Some students will resist your invitation to explore the deeper parts of their souls through the use of these exercises because they know it might hurt to go there.

For example, to imagine God as a loving father could stir up painful reminders of an earthly father who was absent, neglectful, or abusive. To allow Scripture to stir up images of joy and freedom may simply remind students of the lack of these things in their own lives. When kids have experienced painful relationships or traumatic events, they often stuff their deep emotions and lock off portions of their hearts. Some of these exercises will encourage them to expose those scary feelings and explore corners of their hearts that have been hidden until now.

As you lead these exercises, it's your responsibility to monitor your students' responses to what you're asking them to do. If you sense a student is being cautious, please be careful about how hard you push her. If you see a student responding emotionally, offer support and give him permission to disengage if necessary. Sometimes those negative emotions will be intense (anger, sadness, fear, confusion, and so on), and they'll require you to work through things with a student. Be prepared to listen, empathize, encourage—and, if necessary, perhaps even arrange for help beyond what you can offer.—*Marv Penner* (author, speaker, youth ministry professor)

SLOW DOWN

Invite your students to get into a comfortable position—lying down, leaning against a wall, sitting in a chair, and so on. Then help them begin to slow down and let go of whatever distractions may be blocking God's voice. In the sidebar on page 44, "Slow Down," we provide two methods for helping your students do this. You can use them verbatim, adjust them to fit your situation, or do something completely different.

TRANSITION TO IMAGINATIVE PRAYER

Set the scene. "We are at the Sea of Galilee. You can hear the water gently lapping on the shore. A warm breeze is blowing…" Allow the students time to enter the setting. Don't rush this part. Speak slowly and use a number of pauses. The students are using your words to paint a picture, so allow them time for each stroke of their brushes. You may wish to enhance your physical environment with art or with an image projected onto a screen—a picture of a lake, the sound of lapping water, a slight breeze blowing from a quiet fan.

SLOW DOWN

We've used the following two methods and others like them. Notice the common elements: breathing (focus on body); letting go of thoughts, worries, pressures (focus on mind, heart); and prayer (focus moves from self to God). These elements help open us up to what God has for us. Remember: Go slowly! It really does make a difference.

SLOW DOWN #1 (ALLOW THREE TO FIVE MINUTES.)

Say something like—

Once you get into a comfortable position, begin to take slow, deep breaths. Breathe in through your nose and out through your mouth. And inhale enough air so your chest expands.

As you continue taking slow, deep breaths, allow your mind to slow down, letting go of any thoughts and worries. Release the tension in your body. Let the stress flow from your muscles. Allow your body to relax. Continue taking slow, deep breaths—in through your nose and out through your mouth.

As you continue breathing slowly, imagine that God is breathing life, love, and peace into you with each breath you take. As you breathe out, imagine any feelings that are weighing you down—stress, anxiety, and fear—leaving you. Feel yourself sinking deeper and deeper into the presence of God.

Conclude with a silent prayer offering yourself to God, asking God to guide and direct you through this experience.

SLOW DOWN #2 (ALLOW AT LEAST THREE TO FIVE MINUTES.)

(This slow down is similar to the first one. It starts the same way, but it uses hand movements combined with deep breathing.) Say—

Once you get into a comfortable position, begin to take slow, deep breaths. Breathe in through your nose and out through your mouth. And inhale enough air so your chest expands.

As you continue taking slow, deep breaths, allow your mind to slow down, letting go of any thoughts and worries. Release the tension in your body. Let the stress flow from your muscles. Allow your body to relax. Continue taking slow, deep breaths—in through your nose and out through your mouth.

As you continue breathing slowly, turn your hands over—palms down. Imagine yourself dropping those things that are weighing you down: your worries, concerns, and frustrations—those things that bring you emotional discomfort and pain.

When you feel as though you've been able to let these things go, turn your palms up. This represents your readiness to enter into imaginative prayer and receive what God has for you.

Conclude with a silent prayer offering yourself to God, asking God to guide and direct you through this experience.

THE MEDITATION

Again, move slowly. Allow periods of silence. Let your students slowly move through the scene. If, for instance, the meditation invites us to look into the eyes of Jesus, give some time for this. Don't rush to the next thing, but let your students linger here. Trust God during this process. Some say God's favorite language is silence!

LINGERING

Once you've finished the exercise, allow your students to sit quietly with their feelings, impressions, and questions. (Larry refers to this time as "the afterglow.") Don't rush to debrief. This can be an emotionally powerful time, and students need space to reflect on the experience. Provide some silence. But sometimes quiet music or an onscreen image can encourage students to linger with their experiences, rather than feel as though they need to move on to the next thing.

After a few minutes, we usually break the silence by offering a short prayer of thanksgiving. You may enter a time of worship or invite your students to exit the room quietly whenever they're ready. Or you may wish to debrief.

INDIVIDUAL DEBRIEFING

We find it helpful to allow some space for people to individually debrief their experiences. Silence can be very powerful, so resist the natural temptation to break it. In a world of continual noise, the times of silence you provide for your students may help them hear the still, small, loving voice of God for the first time.

You'll need to decide which debriefing methods are most helpful for your group and which will work best with your chosen imaginative prayer exercise. Here are a few ideas to spark your thoughts about individual debriefing. Invite your students to—

- Sit quietly and ponder their experiences
- Each write down one word or phrase they're taking away from the prayer experience and then stick it on the wall of the youth room
- Journal
- Draw, paint, or collage
- Light a candle
- Each place a symbol of their experience before a cross or crucifix
- Use clay to express their experiences

See "Get Creative! More Imaginative Prayer Ideas" (the appendix on page 163) to fill out these ideas and get additional ones. The options are endless.

Ask yourself, *What would be a meaningful way for the students to express what's happened during their prayer experiences?* Make a connection between your debriefing activities and the imaginative prayer exercise. Don't "should" your students! Your goal isn't to have them learn any specific truth, but to help them continue to deepen and build on their experiences. Offer them freedom, safety, and space—a wide-open space for them to be with and hear from God. That is why silence can be so powerful during this time.

You may also wish to provide your students with open-ended prompts or questions for reflection. Put these on a white board or screen, or print them on sheets of paper and pass them out. Here are a few questions that might help you debrief an imaginative prayer experience:

- What were some of your feelings during the exercise? Feelings about you? Feelings about God? About Jesus?

- Did your feelings change as the exercise progressed? If so, how?

- Did anything surprise you? What? How did that affect you?

- What did you feel or sense during your experience?

- What did you feel or sense coming from God?

- What were you drawn to?

- What were you resistant to?

- Do you feel God's invitation to spend more time focusing on something from your experience? What might this be?

Feel free to come up with your own debriefing questions as well. In addition, each exercise in this book contains Optional Journal/Reflection Questions you may want to consider using.

Be careful of the types of questions you ask. Our questions are designed to help people stay in their hearts as they process their thoughts and feelings, not move back into their heads. The questions are open-ended and seek to help students further explore and unpack their experiences to see what they've discovered, embraced, or been invited into by God.

GROUP DEBRIEFING

Don't rush to debrief as a group. (Larry notes that when he's rushed into group debriefing because of limited time, it's caused the experience to be aborted for some people.) Let your students individually and privately respond to God first. Sometimes it's helpful to allow people enough space to take a short walk in silence before debriefing as a group.

YOU HEARD GOD SAY WHAT?

Your students may share something that runs contrary to your view of God. Mentally prepare yourself for this not-so-unlikely scenario.

Picture this: You just led an imaginative prayer exercise and gave time for reflection. You've gathered everyone together for debriefing and things are going extremely well. There is an openness and depth of sharing, there is a feeling that the students are truly listening to each other, the space feels free and safe, and you're feeling pretty good about the whole thing.

Then one of your kids begins to talk. As he shares his experience, uneasiness churns in your gut. You want to interrupt and correct. You imagine your kids all going home with bad theology. You imagine them telling their parents what they learned in church today—and it coming back to haunt you.

Everything in you wants—no needs—to say something. You're the responsible one, so you've got to correct something this misguided, right? Here are some options for you to consider instead:

- **Gently and graciously correct your student's theology publicly, in the moment.** There are a few significant downsides to this option. First, it undermines what you've been trying to create: A safe place where students are free to share their thoughts and experiences. It may shut that student down. It may shut several students down. From that point on, your kids may subconsciously try to say only what you want to hear; and if you're not really careful, you'll limit their openness with you and maybe even with themselves.

   Another downside is that your gut may be wrong. We all "see through a glass, darkly" (1 Corinthians 13:12 KJV), and maybe your student is catching a reflection of God you simply haven't seen before. Be very careful to not make little ones stumble and diminish their desire to hear from God personally.

- **Ask the student for clarification.** Maybe it's not really as bad as you think! Maybe the student is still roaming safely within the spacious confines of orthodoxy. But avoid asking for clarification only when you disagree with someone or else the safety and openness of the debriefing environment will diminish over time. Sometimes it's best to just move on to the next person.

- **Set up a time to talk with the student privately or chat after the meeting.** It may help to have some time to consider how to approach your student so you're not just reacting in the moment. Plus, this won't harm the safe, open, sharing space you're trying to maintain. Then listen for more of who your student is and learn what her image of God might be. A bit of wonder is a good thing. Try to avoid an agenda to correct.

If you create a safe space, then kids will talk. And what they say at times may be shocking. So think through your own ministry setting and personal convictions, and decide ahead of time how you'll try to respond when a kid says something that doesn't sit well with your theology.

Questions, such as those listed previously and in the Optional Journal/Reflection Questions sections, can also be used for group debriefing. One note of caution: Deeply personal questions are usually best left for individual reflection rather than group debriefing.

Still, group sharing can be very meaningful. Speaking aloud about something you've experienced can make it more real to you. Hearing about someone else's experience can help you arrive at a new truth for yourself. However, we offer another caution: These spoken words can sometimes take us from our hearts and put us back into our heads—and quite abruptly.

If you choose to move into group sharing, it's important to encourage and welcome all kinds of experiences—even if nothing seems to have happened. Remember to stress to your students that imaginative prayer is a way to offer ourselves to God, who is always present—it doesn't cause God to show up. And remind them that even if it feels like absolutely nothing happened, God is still working in us in ways we cannot understand or feel.

A CAUTION ABOUT GROUP DEBRIEFING (PLEASE READ THIS!)

Some of your students may be in very fragile and vulnerable places. They've opened themselves up to God and may have powerfully experienced God's presence. This can lead to a great realization of their belovedness, much like John the Apostle. Or they may come face-to-face with their brokenness like Isaiah. Be gentle. Create a safe place for your students to debrief as a group. How?

- Give absolute freedom to share or not share—stress the value and benefits of both.

- Don't allow cross talking. No one is free to comment on what's been shared—neither during the sharing time, nor afterward.

- Instruct the group that after someone has shared, they're to hold up that person and her words to God in silent prayer for a few moments.

FINAL COMMENTS

Make sure you and your staff members are available to talk with students one-on-one—either now or later in the week. Encourage students to revisit this experience or passage and see if God has more for them to discover. Remind them of the value of writing down what they felt, experienced, and learned about themselves and God.

SECTION THREE
WHAT?

CHAPTER 7

IMAGES OF GOD [FIVE EXERCISES]

GOD AS EAGLE

Scripture References: Exodus 19:4; Deuteronomy 32:10-11; Psalm 57:1

Themes: Confusion, Rescue, Trust

SNEAK PEEK

The Bible uses the eagle to describe God. This exercise leads students into the experience of learning how to fly.

BELLS AND WHISTLES

- Imaginative Prayer Treasure Chest (refer to page 37)
- Pictures of eagles soaring
- Aerial nature scenes
- Sound track of wind

RUNDOWN

1. Slow Down (refer to page 44)
2. Read Imaginative Prayer Meditation.
3. Offer students quiet space for reflection.
4. Optional Reflection/Journal Questions

IMAGINATIVE PRAYER MEDITATION

You're a baby eagle, an eaglet. Your mother is big and strong with wings so wide she lets you ride on top of them. You're soaring high above the world on the wings of your mother eagle. The wind is against your face as you fly toward the sun. This is amazing! It's exciting and wonderful to be held up by your mother, the one who protects you, feeds you, and loves you. You sing in the safety of those wings. You feel the wind and the sun and look at the beauty below and above and around you. **(Pause a moment.)**

Remember how fiercely your mother protects you from harm. You are her delight, the apple of her eye. When threats are near, she hides you within her wings. You feel safe in that warm place, in that shadow. You cling to her, and she doesn't let you fall. She shields you, cares for you, and guards you. Allow yourself to enjoy feeling loved and protected. **(Pause a moment.)**

Suddenly your mother flips over and you fall. Your small body is rushing toward the ground! Your mind freezes. You're helpless. You're going to hit the earth! **(Pause a moment.)** Then you stop falling. Your mother spreads her wings beneath you, catches you, and breaks your fall. You're very confused, and you have no idea what just happened, but it felt horrible. Now your mother flies high into the sky, and just as you begin to catch your breath, she flips again—and you're falling again! She's doing this on purpose! Why? Does she want you to die? Does she think it's funny? What could she be thinking? **(Pause a moment.)**

Again, as you plummet toward the earth, your mother spreads her wings beneath you and stops your fall. You're in tears, totally confused.

As she soars high into the sky, she looks back at you. Your mother's face is as fiercely loving and protective as always. "Flap your wings, dear child," she says, then she flips yet again and allows you to fall.

OPTIONAL REFLECTION/JOURNAL QUESTIONS

- What emotions come up for you as you fall? As you realize your mother is purposefully causing your fall?

- Does the fact that she's teaching you to fly make it okay? Why or why not?

- Do you feel safe with this mother as your protector? Do you feel safe with God? Why or why not?

- Remember a time when you found yourself confused and disoriented like the baby eagle in freefall—what was that like for you? What was your experience of God during that time?

- Do you feel as though you're falling now? Share your honest thoughts and feelings with God.

[End]

GOD AS MOTHER

Scripture References: Psalm 131; Isaiah 66:13; Zephaniah 3:17

Themes: Rest, Loved by God, Comforted

SNEAK PEEK

God is depicted as mother in Scripture. This exercise invites your students to experience themselves as distressed infants being comforted and rocked by their loving Mother God.

BELLS AND WHISTLES

- Imaginative Prayer Treasure Chest (refer to page 37)
- Pillows and blankets
- Quiet lullaby music
- Darkened room

RUNDOWN

1. Invite students to lie down; if you have blankets and pillows, pass them out.
2. Slow Down (refer to page 44)
3. Read Imaginative Prayer Meditation
4. Offer students quiet space for reflection.
5. Optional Reflection/Journal Questions

IMAGINATIVE PRAYER MEDITATION

You are an infant, lying in your tiny crib. Waking suddenly in the night, you feel frightened and begin to cry. Your body tenses up. You're alone and disoriented. You don't know what's wrong, but you cry because something is. Feel your frustration, fear, and helplessness. **(Pause a moment.)**

A soft voice comes out of the darkness, and gentle hands pick you up. "Hush, my baby, mommy's here." Your body begins to relax as your mother sings over you and rocks you back and forth, back and forth. Your tears stop, and you snuggle into the warmth of your mother's arms.

Your worries and fears are gone now. Nothing concerns you. There's nothing you need. Rest in the arms of your mother, your head pressed against her chest. You hear the rhythmic beating of her heart and feel her chest gently rising and falling with each breath she takes. You're completely safe and perfectly loved. **(Pause a moment.)**

As you continue to rest, gently change your perspective. This is not your physical mother who rocks and holds you so lovingly. This is God, your Mother. God, the Life-Giver and Nurturer, holds you gently, enveloping you in love. God, your Mother, wipes your tears and smiles while gazing into the beautiful face of her beloved child.

Rest in the arms of your Mother. Rest in the arms of God.

OPTIONAL REFLECTION/JOURNAL QUESTIONS

- What's it like for you to consider God as a mother? How does that feel for you?

- What happens when you picture yourself as an distressed baby?

- How does it feel to be picked up, held, and comforted by God, your Mother?

- What happens when you picture God singing to you and smiling with delight when she looks into your face?

- Share your thoughts and feelings with God. Listen for the song God sings over you.

[End]

GOD AS POTTER

Scripture Reference: Isaiah 64:8

Themes: Loved by God, Significance

SNEAK PEEK

God is depicted as a potter, and we are the clay that's being shaped into a pot. Your students are invited to see themselves as lovingly created by the One who creates and views them with delight. Let the students discover this for themselves while they go through the exercise.

BELLS AND WHISTLES

- Imaginative Prayer Treasure Chest (refer to page 37)

- Have students take pieces of clay to mold for individual reflection time

- Pottery or pictures of pottery to display

- A potter's wheel; or arrange to have a potter present during the exercise to either act out the meditation or throw (form or shape) a pot when the meditation ends

RUNDOWN

1. Slow Down (refer to page 44)

2. Tell your students you'll be reading the meditation twice.

3. Read Imaginative Prayer Meditation.

4. Offer students quiet space for reflection.

5. Read Imaginative Prayer Meditation again, inviting your students to enter the scene, picturing themselves as the clay.

6. Offer students quiet space for reflection. If you choose to provide clay, now would be the time to invite students to take some to mold.

7. Optional Reflection/Journal Questions

IMAGINATIVE PRAYER MEDITATION

The room is simple: A concrete floor, some clay, and a potter's wheel. There's a large window. A ray of sun shines across the floor. A potter sits at the wheel. She sets a lump of clay on the wheel, and the wheel begins to spin.

The potter's hands dance with the clay, interacting lovingly with it. She sings over the clay while delicately and expertly creating her art. The song is specific to this piece of clay. Her words speak of beauty and life, joy and hope, purpose and infinite value. This is no ordinary pot she's creating. This is a masterpiece.

As the clay begins to take shape, she laughs with delight. Her face glows with joy. When she's finished, she holds her creation high as if in triumph. Then the potter brings her creation very close to her face. She touches it to her cheek. "Perfect," she whispers.

"We are the clay, you are the potter; we are all the work of your hand" (Isaiah 64:8).

OPTIONAL REFLECTION/JOURNAL QUESTIONS

- How does it feel to know that you're a created masterpiece and the Potter planned you in great detail?

- Do you feel like a masterpiece? Why or why not?

- Listen as you're held up to the Potter's cheek and proclaimed "perfect."

- Talk to God, your Potter, and tell God how you feel about how you've been made.

[End]

GOD AS RESCUER

Scripture Reference: Psalm 18

Themes: Rescue, Loved by God, Identity

SNEAK PEEK

Psalm 18 depicts God's visually over-the-top rescue of the psalmist. In this exercise your students are invited to experience that rescue as their own.

BELLS AND WHISTLES

- Imaginative Prayer Treasure Chest (refer to page 37)

- Sound track or visual media of a peaceful meadow setting, switching to a dark storm, and back to the peaceful meadow—timed to go along with the meditation

- Pillows and blankets

RUNDOWN

1. Invite students to lie down; if you have blankets and pillows, pass them out.

2. Slow Down (refer to page 44)

3. Read Imaginative Prayer Meditation.

4. Offer students quiet space for reflection.

5. Optional Reflection/Journal Questions

IMAGINATIVE PRAYER MEDITATION

You open your eyes and look around. You sit up, not knowing where you are or how you got here. You're on the edge of a spacious meadow. There's a stream nearby and flowers everywhere. You hear birds and see butterflies. A grove of trees partly shades you from the sun.

You slowly realize you're not alone. You've actually been resting on a comforting lap. Looking into the eyes of your Comforter, into the eyes of God, you ask the question on your mind: "How am I safe? I was drowning…"

God smiles and helps you lie down again. You close your eyes as God strokes your hair and begins to speak, "You were in the middle of the stormy ocean. The waves surrounded you, and you were about to go under for the last time. I saw you, and I rescued you."

You slowly remember a crazy and unbelievable scene: The sky is dark, the waves are rough. Your stomach tightems with fear as you frantically tread water, gulp it down, and sink. You feel the numbing cold. **(Pause a moment.)** You taste the choking saltiness. **(Pause a moment.)** Your confused mind is frozen in fear, knowing your strength is gone, and you're about to drown. **(Pause a moment.)** Then a powerful earthquake shakes the mountains. God appears, and smoke billows from God's nostrils. You see fire come from God's mouth as God's voice thunders from heaven. God splits open the sky and flies on the wings of the wind to your rescue. Strong hands reach down and take hold of you, pulling you from the deep waters. You struggle to catch your breath as shock mixes with fear and exhaustion. You lose consciousness as you're lifted to safety. **(Pause a moment.)**

As your mind returns to the peace of the meadow, God gently says, "I brought you to this spacious place. I rescued you because you are my delight, my child, my love. Rest now, dear one. You are safe."

OPTIONAL REFLECTION/JOURNAL QUESTIONS

- Picture the God in this meditation, the God whose voice and breath move the ocean. Compose the feelings that arise within you as you hear God's powerful voice.

- Can you believe God would move all of nature to rescue you?

- Can you imagine how important you must be to God? What thoughts and feelings come up for you? Share them with God.

- Picture God gently holding your head and inviting you to rest. What emotions does this image of God bring up for you? How do the words *you are safe* make you feel? What do they mean to you?

- How do you feel when you're told that you are God's delight, God's child, God's love? Share your thoughts and feelings with God. Hear God repeat those words to you again.

[End]

GOD AS SHEPHERD

Scripture Reference: Psalm 23

Themes: God's Care, Safety, Peace

SNEAK PEEK

God is depicted as one who shepherds us. This exercise invites students to enjoy the care of their Shepherd.

BELLS AND WHISTLES

- Imaginative Prayer Treasure Chest (refer to page 37)

- Visual nature scenes (meadow, stream)

- Audio nature sounds

RUNDOWN

1. Slow Down (refer to page 44)

2. Tell students you'll be reading the meditation twice.

3. Read Imaginative Prayer Meditation, inviting students to focus on the *gifts* offered to them in the scene.

4. Offer students quiet space for reflection.

5. Read Imaginative Prayer Meditation a second time, inviting students to focus on the *Giver* of the gifts.

6. Offer students quiet space for reflection.

7. Optional Reflection/Journal Questions

IMAGINATIVE PRAYER MEDITATION

Walking hand in hand with God, you're led through green meadows so you can lie down and rest when you're tired. You feel safe…comfortable…relaxed. Feel the cool breeze against your skin and the warm sun on your face. Breathe in deeply the peace God offers you. Someone watches over you while you sleep. Rest a moment. **(Pause a moment.)**

God—the Creator of *all* of this—is good. God is the One who takes care of you so everything you need is yours. When you feel thirsty, God leads you to a fresh stream. Feel the cool water, taste its sweetness. **(Pause a moment.)**

Your soul is restored and refreshed as you journey with God. You are gently guided along paths that offer life to you and to others, paths of good things. Your heart is full. You really want to sing. Go ahead. **(Pause a moment.)**

Even when you walk through a dark, scary valley, there is nothing to fear. God is with you, protecting and comforting you. You'll never be left alone. Feel yourself lifted into God's strong arms as you journey through the dark. **(Pause a moment.)**

God prepares a banquet for you in the midst of all your fears. You are God's own. God blesses you with oil. Your joy overflows as you sit at the table and eat. **(Pause a moment.)**

Goodness and love will be with you always. You'll live in the house of love forever and ever. Stay in the beauty of this love that never ends. Dance, play, rest. Enjoy.

OPTIONAL REFLECTION/JOURNAL QUESTIONS

- Which part of the meditation resonated with you the most? Why?

- Spend time imagining yourself in that place again. Share your heart with God. Allow God to nurture you.

- Was there any part of the meditation you found difficult? Spend some time considering that with God.

- Do you sense an invitation from God? How are you drawn to respond?

[End]

CHAPTER 8

O.T. TIME [EIGHT EXERCISES]

GOD SEES HAGAR

Scripture Reference: Genesis 16:6-13

Themes: Powerlessness, Rescue

SNEAK PEEK

Hagar is abused by Sarai and runs away. Out in the desert, God tells Hagar to go back to Sarai, and also gives her promises about her life to come. The story doesn't end neatly. God doesn't deal directly with the subject of abuse, nor does God remove Hagar from the situation. But God sees Hagar, cares about her, and lets her know she'll be okay.

BELLS AND WHISTLES

- Imaginative Prayer Treasure Chest (refer to page 37)
- A desert visual

RUNDOWN

1. Slow Down (refer to page 44)

2. Read Imaginative Prayer Meditation.

3. Offer students quiet space for reflection.

4. Optional Reflection/Journal Questions

IMAGINATIVE PRAYER MEDITATION

You're a woman and a servant. You have no rights of your own. The woman you serve, Sarai, has no children. So she gave you to her husband, Abram, hoping you'd get pregnant for her and have a child for her. In your culture this is not uncommon. It is, however, complicated. Now you're pregnant, and Sarai is jealous. She's mean and abusive, so you run away.

Your world is a desert. After walking for three days, you're nearly out of water and food. You're dirty and very tired. You've had no shelter, and no help is expected. Even if you should meet someone, no one wants a pregnant servant. You're probably running to your death.

You see a spring of water and drop down beside it in gratitude. The water is fresh and cold and sweet. You drink and drink until your stomach is full, and you stay there to rest. But there is no peace in your soul. You begin to cry tears of anger and frustration. "God, where are you? This is so unfair. I didn't ask for any of this! Why did you let this happen? Why is there no one to protect me?"

Suddenly, you hear your name. "Hagar." God is standing before you. "Hagar, what are you doing here?" God's eyes see inside you. You can barely return the gaze, yet you cannot turn away. "I'm running away. Don't you know I was being mistreated?" you say.

God bends down and touches your cheek. "Yes, I know. I see. Go back," God says. "Go back. It'll be okay. You're not alone there. I am with you, and I won't ever leave you."

As God looks into your eyes, time seems to stop. The very God of the world is looking at you, looking into you, and knowing you. You've never been in such an intimate space before; you're in awe.

Then it's over, and God is gone. You touch your cheek where God's hand had been. What did God say? To go back to the people who mistreated you—but God promised to be with you.

This is not the rescue you wanted. Express your feelings to God.

OPTIONAL REFLECTION/JOURNAL QUESTIONS

- Do you feel seen by God? Why or why not?

- Do you need rescue or protection in some way? You're invited to share your heart with God.

- God's rescue for Hagar wasn't what she wanted. Is there some way God is taking care of you that isn't what you had in mind? Talk to God about that.

[End]

HANNAH'S CRY

Scripture Reference: 1 Samuel 1:1-28

Themes: Faith, Honesty

SNEAK PEEK

The exercise is inspired by Hannah's tearful cry to God for a son. Sometimes we have deep desires, and God invites us to open our hearts and share them with him. In this exercise your students are invited to do this.

BELLS AND WHISTLES

- Imaginative Prayer Treasure Chest (refer to page 37)

- Altar, icons, cross, or crucifix; anything that lends itself to a temple feel

- A darkened room

- Incense or candles burning

RUNDOWN

1. Slow Down (refer to page 44)

2. Read Imaginative Prayer Meditation.

3. Offer students quiet space for reflection. If you've created an altar space, then you may wish to invite your students to come to the altar as they pray and talk to God.

4. Optional Reflection/Journal Questions

IMAGINATIVE PRAYER MEDITATION

You're sitting in the temple. It's quiet in here, and the light is just beginning to fade. The fragrance of sacrifices is strong. The air is thick with incense. It's peaceful, yet you don't feel any peace. Your heart is full of pain. That's why you're here. You've come to the temple to find God and beg for help.

A woman enters the temple. She's staggering and nearly falls to her knees. She looks the way you feel. She sways back and forth a while, but eventually her body is still. She stays there so long you begin to think she's asleep, except her mouth is moving. You wonder if she's mentally ill or drunk.

You're not alone in your wondering. The priest of the temple walks over and accuses her of being drunk. The poor woman is crying inconsolably. No, she hasn't been drinking. She's very upset. And she's been pouring her heart out, telling God her deepest pains and deepest desires. She's been laying her longings before God, begging God for mercy, begging God to hear her prayer and grant her request. The priest blesses her, and she leaves. As she walks past, you notice a smile on her face.

As her footfalls fade, the temple becomes silent once more. Out of this silence you hear—or perhaps you feel—a voice. It's God's voice. "What are your deepest pains and deepest desires? Will you pour your heart out to me, too? Will you lay your longings before me?"

And now it is silent again.

OPTIONAL REFLECTION/JOURNAL QUESTIONS

- Spend time in the temple with God. Tell God whatever's on your heart.

- Notice your body's response. Do you want to leave or stay?

- What is your reaction to God's questions? What feelings do they uncover and release within you?

- The woman left with a smile on her face. Perhaps she felt heard and that helped her to leave with a lighter heart. Do you feel heard by God? If so, how does that make you feel? If not, how does that make you feel?

[End]

ELIJAH RESTS AND EATS

Scripture References: 1 Kings 18:30-40; 19:1-7

Themes: Depression, Fear, Worries, Rest

SNEAK PEEK

We've included two exercises on Elijah. They can either be used together or separately. In this exercise Elijah is afraid and he feels abandoned. He's exhausted, and he's given up. So God tells him to eat. After he eats, Elijah lies down and rests. Sometimes we need to do the same. Your students are invited to enter this story and receive God's provision for them just as Elijah does. The exercise called *God Whispers to Elijah*, on page 67, continues the narrative.

BELLS AND WHISTLES

- Imaginative Prayer Treasure Chest (refer to page 37)

- Pillows and blankets

- A snack (this option could be cool, but it might also be disruptive). If you plan to use this exercise after your students have done or been through something as a group—something physically or emotionally exhausting—then a much-needed snack or even cups of cool water might be a good addition to the meditation.

- Desert visual

RUNDOWN

1. Slow Down (refer to page 44)

2. Read Imaginative Prayer Meditation.

3. Pass out any pillows, blankets, or snack items as God invites Elijah to rest and eat.

4. Offer students quiet space for reflection.

5. Optional Reflection/Journal Questions

IMAGINATIVE PRAYER MEDITATION

You are an observer of this scene. Out in the hot and dry desert, you're sitting under a bush that somehow protects you from the worst of the heat. You see a man coming your way. He looks exhausted. He walks without looking where he's going. He also seems to be talking to himself. The man approaches another bush, not far from you, and flings himself under it. You hear him crying and talking.

This is what you're able to hear: "God, I've loved you, and I've obeyed you. I've risked so much for you, always doing everything you ask me to do. I've suffered for you; many people have rejected me because of my obedience to you. You've also shown me wonderful things, and you've let me be a part of some cool stuff. You've even given me joy and peace. Only now—none of it seems to matter. I'm exhausted and afraid. I feel totally alone. Are you there, God? I'm running for my life. People are chasing me and trying to kill me! I'm starving and thirsty and tired. I can't stop shaking. I can't do this anymore. I'm done! Just let me die!"

Lying down, the man continues to whimper for a few moments; then his breathing deepens, and he falls asleep.

Suddenly, the man isn't alone. Someone has appeared right next to him. The visitor builds a small fire and bakes some bread. When that's finished, the visitor kneels by the sleeping man and gently shakes him awake. When the man sees the visitor's face, he cries, "I don't know what to do. I don't know where to go. Oh, God, please help me!"

God responds, "Eat. That's all you need to do right now. I know everything feels overwhelming. It's okay. Take a break and have some food. When you've regained your strength, then I'll show you the next thing. Then God disappears. The man sits up and sees the bread and a jug of water. He eats, drinks, and falls back asleep.

You turn away from the man and see God is now kneeling next to you and preparing another loaf of bread. God turns to you and smiles. God picks up the loaf of bread and a jug of water and offers it to you. "Rest and eat," God says. "That's all you need to do right now. Just rest and eat. Don't worry or try to figure anything out. Just rest and eat." Then God disappears.

Spend some time receiving God's invitation. Rest and eat. Simply "be."

OPTIONAL REFLECTION/JOURNAL QUESTIONS

- How do you respond when you're afraid, overwhelmed, exhausted?

- Can you remember a time when life was overwhelming? Do you feel that way now?

- Do you need to give yourself time to regain your strength? Do you need to spend some time accepting God's invitation to just be?

- What emotions come up for you as you enter this story, as you experience Elijah's pain and fear and confusion?

- As you hear God's invitation to let go of your worries and just rest and eat, what happens inside you? How does this make you feel about God?

- What was it like to have God serve you?

- Imagine God serving you again. How does it make you feel?

[End]

GOD WHISPERS TO ELIJAH

Scripture Reference: 1 Kings 19:8-13

Themes: Confusion, Guidance

SNEAK PEEK

This is the second of two exercises we've written about Elijah. They can either be used together or separately. In this one Elijah has just rested and regained his strength (which is the focus of *Elijah Rests and Eats* on page 64). Now he's ready to find out what God wants to say to him, where God wishes to lead him next. As God speaks to Elijah, your students are invited to listen as God speaks to them as well.

BELLS AND WHISTLES

- Imaginative Prayer Treasure Chest (refer to page 37)
- A visual of Mount Horeb or another mountain

RUNDOWN

1. Slow Down (refer to page 44)
2. Read Imaginative Prayer Meditation.
3. Offer students quiet space for reflection.
4. Optional Reflection/Journal Questions

IMAGINATIVE PRAYER MEDITATION

You wake up under a bush in the desert. Coming out of a sound sleep, you find yourself rested. You sit up and stretch, and then you see a man sitting nearby. You observe him. He doesn't seem to see you. He begins to walk, and you follow him.

The two of you walk for a very long time. It's totally silent, except for an occasional cry from the man ahead of you: "God, where are you? Where do you want me to go? What do you want for my life? Please talk to me, God. I'm confused and afraid. Don't leave me alone!" You're left wondering some of the same things and wondering if God will answer the man. Wondering if God will answer you.

You and the man begin to climb. You climb and climb until you reach the top of a mountain. The man asks God to speak to him. You wait for God to speak, too.

A great and powerful wind tears the mountains apart and shatters the rocks; but as you listen, you don't hear God in the wind. Where is God?

Then an earthquake shakes the foundations of the mountain; but as you listen, you don't hear God in the earthquake. Where is God? A fire from heaven consumes the ground and the heat is almost unbearable; but as you listen, you don't hear God in the fire. Where is God?

As you and the man listen, you hear a gentle whisper and he falls to the ground with hands raised. You continue to listen. God is in the whisper. God—who made the wind, earthquake, and fire—speaks your name in a gentle whisper. "What are you doing here?" God asks.

You're invited to share with God all that's on your heart. And then in the quiet, turn your ear toward God's whisper and listen. What do you want to whisper to God? What does God want to say to you?

OPTIONAL REFLECTION/JOURNAL QUESTIONS

- What were your whispers to God?

- What was God's whisper to you?

- Do you have a place of confusion, pain, or joy to share with God? If so, take time to share the whispering of your heart with God.

[End]

ESTHER'S COURAGE

Scripture Reference: Esther 1–10

Themes: Courage, Justice

SNEAK PEEK

This is the story of Purim, the story of God's rescue of the Hebrew people. It's written from the perspective of Esther, a Hebrew woman chosen to live in the king's harem and faced with a very difficult decision. She must decide whether or not to risk her own life for the sake of justice for her people.

BELLS AND WHISTLES

- Imaginative Prayer Treasure Chest (refer to page 37)
- Pillows and blankets
- Darkened room

RUNDOWN

1. Slow Down (refer to page 44)
2. Read Imaginative Prayer Meditation.
3. Offer students quiet space for reflection as indicated in the exercise.
4. Optional Reflection/Journal Questions

IMAGINATIVE PRAYER MEDITATION

Your name is Esther. You live in the palace of the king as his queen. Life is usually very good here. There are wonderful clothes and delicious food, and you can have almost anything you want. It's a dream come true.

There are some rules here in the palace. No one can talk to the king unless he talks to that person first. No one may see the king unless he asks that person to come to him. Breaking these rules can get you killed. But you've never been tempted to break them—until now.

Lying in your bed, you can't sleep. Your brain is busy worrying. The king has signed a law that will get all the Jews in the country killed. Haman is the evil man who's planning this horrible plot. Does the king understand what he's agreed to? You're not sure. If you go to the king and beg for mercy for the Jews, you may be killed, too. But if you don't, all the Jewish people certainly will die. Time is running out.

You wonder if God had something to do with you becoming queen. You wonder if the reason God put you here in the palace was so you could speak for justice right now. The knot in your stomach is making you nauseated, and you can taste your fear. A prayer falls from your lips, "Please help, please help, please help."

Take time to feel the weight of the decision you have to make. **(Allow significant pause.)**

Esther did approach the king, the king repealed the law, and the Jews were saved. Today, Jews celebrate the time when God rescued them from the hate of Haman. The holiday is called Purim, and it's the happiest of all Jewish celebrations.

OPTIONAL REFLECTION/JOURNAL QUESTIONS

- Have you ever wondered if you were put in a certain place so you could help someone in need? How did you respond to that situation?

- Who in your life and world needs you to seek justice for them? How can you do that?

- What feelings arise in you when you see people mistreated or suffering unjustly? How are you drawn to respond?

[End]

THE DESPERATE CRY

Scripture References: Various Psalms

Themes: Powerlessness, Suffering, Honesty

SNEAK PEEK

A compilation of psalms that bluntly tell it like it is, express raw pain and suffering, and ask God to come to the rescue.

BELLS AND WHISTLES

- Imaginative Prayer Treasure Chest (refer to page 37)

- A darkened room, simple and sterile

RUNDOWN

1. Slow Down (refer to page 44)

2. Read Imaginative Prayer Meditation, telling your students beforehand that the meditation is compiled from the Psalms. Invite your students to enter the meditation and experience the words for themselves.

3. Offer students quiet space for reflection.

4. Optional Reflection/Journal Questions

IMAGINATIVE PRAYER MEDITATION

Desperate, alone, and afraid, you hide in a cave. You've been here a long time. It's dark, cold, and damp. The ground is hard. Your clothes are thin and torn and dirty.

In your pain, you cry to God: "I am empty. My bones ache and grow weak. Tears have been my only food. My heart is broken, and my mouth is dried up. My eyes grow weak with sorrow, my soul and body with grief. I lie here and groan. There is no comfort. No one comes to help me. I am utterly alone, forgotten as though I were already dead. My heart pounds, my strength fails me; there is no light, only darkness. All I hear, see, smell, and taste is pain and death. I cannot speak. I have no voice. My screaming is silent, yet so loud inside my head. Am I going crazy? My heart is anxious and worried. I'm afraid of death but afraid of life, too. There is horror everywhere for me. I can't stop shaking. I'm lost."

Sit silently and feel the unspoken pain of your soul. If there are more or different words or feelings you'd like to share with God, take this time to do that as well. **(Allow significant pause.)**

As the meditation continues, you're invited to remain in this place of pain and to tell God what you need and want—to ask for rescue.

"Help me and rescue me from dying. See me and hear my silent cries. Don't let me go crazy; calm my heart. Be my safe place. I'm calling to you. Can you hear me? You're my only hope. If you don't hear me, if you don't answer, if I'm left alone, then I'll die. Lord, my faithful God, have mercy. Find me and save me. My life is in your hands. Deliver me. God, do not reject me; do not be far away. Hurry to help me, my Lord and my Savior. Listen to my prayer."

OPTIONAL REFLECTION/JOURNAL QUESTIONS

- What does it feel like to be desperate and powerless? Do you know what it's like to silently scream? If so, tell God about that.

- Have you ever expressed your pain like this?

- Were you able to express your suffering to God? If not, take time now to express to God your feelings of pain. What was that experience like?

- Where is God when you're in pain, lonely, or afraid? Does God seem close or far away? You're invited to talk to God about that.

- When you're struggling, do you cry to God for help?

- Have you ever experienced being rescued from danger? What was that like for you?

[End]

A NEW NAME

Scripture Reference: Isaiah 62:1-12

Themes: Identity, Loved by God, Significance

SNEAK PEEK

Isaiah 62 has been adapted for the following exercise. The passage is beautiful, leaving us overwhelmed by God's lavish words of love for us. We hope this exercise will leave your students sensing their own deep value as well. However, be aware of the fact that it may also bring up pain for those students who cannot receive these words.

BELLS AND WHISTLES

- Imaginative Prayer Treasure Chest (refer to page 37)

- Handheld mirrors for each person to look into while listening to God's words

- Ambient music

- Print out the words of the meditation for your students to take home with them.

RUNDOWN

1. Tell your students you'll read through the meditation twice.

2. Slow Down (refer to page 44). This exercise is short and it starts right in, so the Slow Down is especially important to help your students get into a quiet, receptive posture.

3. Read Imaginative Prayer Meditation, inviting your students to hear the words spoken by God to each one of them.

4. Offer students quiet space for reflection.

5. Reread the Imaginative Prayer Meditation and give the students more time for reflection.

6. Optional Reflection/Journal Questions

IMAGINATIVE PRAYER MEDITATION

I can't stop talking about you. I can't stop thinking about you.

Your beauty and righteousness will be seen throughout the world.

Kings will be in awe of you.

You'll be seen as a priceless crown held in my hand, a stunning jewel, marvelous to see.

Never again will you be called Rejected. Never again will you be called Worthless.

You'll be called My Delight, My Joy.

I'll give you your true name, your secret name that only I know. I'll whisper it to you.

So stand up and know who you are, my Precious One, my Shining Star, my Beloved.

Comb your hair and wash your face and be glad.

OPTIONAL REFLECTION/JOURNAL QUESTIONS

- What's it like to hear those words spoken about you and to you?
- Are they easy or difficult to receive? Why?
- Do any of these words from God feel especially important for you to hear?

[End]

DANIEL AND THE LIONS' DEN

Scripture Reference: Daniel 6:1-28

Themes: Trust, Courage, Love for God

SNEAK PEEK

Daniel chooses to pray and maintain his intimacy with God—even when it puts his life in danger. Your students are invited to journey with Daniel and consider the love and trust Daniel has for God, as well as the love and trust they experience with God themselves.

BELLS AND WHISTLES

- Imaginative Prayer Treasure Chest (refer to page 37)
- Visual of an open window

RUNDOWN

1. Slow Down (refer to page 44)
2. Read Imaginative Prayer Meditation.
3. Offer students quiet space for reflection.
4. Optional Reflection/Journal Questions

IMAGINATIVE PRAYER MEDITATION

You're a young man named Daniel. Your country lost a war, and you've been taken far away from your home. Your family was separated, as were your friends' families. In your loneliness, God has been very present. And your prayer life has become so important. You pray three times every day with your windows open toward home. God hears as you share your confusion and sadness, as well as your joys and successes.

You feel pretty alone in this new land, so you seem to turn to God even more fully. God speaks to you in dreams, sending you messages and telling you what will happen in the future. It's been kind of freaky, especially when all the dreams come true. You love God, and you love your relationship with God. Your trust in God is really strong.

One day that trust is tested. A law is passed that makes it illegal to pray to anyone but the king for 30 days. Those who disobey this law will be thrown into the lions' den to die a horrible death.

What do you do? Spend some time with this question. Search your heart and talk to God about your answer. Ask God to help you see your true heart. Remember, God loves and accepts you just where you are, no matter what your answer is. Notice what feelings come up for you while considering this choice. **(Allow significant pause.)**

If you choose to break the new law and continue praying to God, then continue to place yourself in the story as Daniel. If you choose to obey the law and set aside your prayer for the next 30 days, you're invited to become an observer in the story and watch what happens to Daniel. **(Pause a moment.)**

Daniel continues to pray to God. His prayer life is the most important part of who he is, and he can't imagine setting it aside—even for 30 days. So three times a day, Daniel opens his windows toward his homeland and prays within sight and sound of anyone who walks by.

Soon, Daniel is caught praying to God, and he's brought before the king. As the law commands, Daniel must be condemned and thrown into the lions' den. Even though Daniel has been obedient to God, he's also been condemned to death for it.

That night Daniel is thrown to the lions and the cave is sealed shut. It's completely dark and the smell in the cave is terrible. Daniel can hear the lions breathing and pacing restlessly. He senses how hungry they are. Spend some time in that cave. Where is God? What are you feeling? **(Allow significant pause.)**

God keeps Daniel safe throughout the night. Do you wonder if he was afraid or if he experienced peace? How would you have felt? And how would you feel the next morning when you were still alive? What would happen to your trust in God?

OPTIONAL REFLECTION/JOURNAL QUESTIONS

- Have you ever really trusted God for something? How did that turn out for you? Is there something you're trusting God for now? If so, what is it?

- Can you imagine making the same decision Daniel did? Why or why not?

- How does loneliness impact your relationship with God?

- When you feel alone, what questions arise within you? Bring your questions to God.

[End]

CHAPTER 9

GOSPEL TIME — ADVENT [TWO EXERCISES]

MARY'S PREGNANT

Scripture Reference: Luke 1:26-38

Theme: Faith

SNEAK PEEK

This exercise invites your students to view themselves as being pregnant with Jesus and asks them to explore what it would mean to give birth to Jesus in the everyday events of their lives.

BELLS AND WHISTLES

- Imaginative Prayer Treasure Chest (refer to page 37)

RUNDOWN

1. Read the entire account (Luke 1:26-38) to your students as a backdrop for the exercise.

2. Read Imaginative Prayer Meditation—Part One.

3. Slow Down (refer to page 44)

4. Read Imaginative Prayer Meditation—Part Two.

5. Offer students quiet space for reflection.

6. Optional Reflection/Journal Questions

IMAGINATIVE PRAYER MEDITATION — PART ONE

Just like in the story about Mary, an angel will visit you in this meditation. But before we begin, let's create the place where this encounter will happen. It can be wherever you choose, inside or outside, the mountains, the beach, the desert, or by a lake or rushing river. The actual location doesn't matter just as long as it feels safe and comfortable to you.

Take a few moments to create your setting; pay attention to the sounds and the temperature. Are you sitting, lying down, or standing? If you're outside, is there a breeze? Is the sky clear or cloudy? If you're inside, are you on a couch or seated in a big comfortable chair? Are there windows? If so, are they open or closed? Is it daytime? Is it cold outside? Is there a fireplace? Is there a fire? Remember, whatever you decide, you should make it a place where you feel comfortable and safe.

(Once the students are settled, walk them through the *Slow Down* on page 44).

IMAGINATIVE PRAYER MEDITATION — PART TWO

Imagine you're now in the place you've created. You're enjoying your surroundings, resting and relaxing without a trouble or worry in the world. You feel at ease, peaceful, and calm.

Then an angel of the Lord appears to you. The angel speaks, "Greetings, favored one, the Lord is with you." Sit with these words, think about them. Are they easy for you to believe, to receive? How do they make you feel? **(Allow significant pause.)**

The angel continues, "God has decided to bless you. You and God will be on the same team, partners, working together. You're pregnant and will give birth."

You're confused. "Pregnant? But how can this be?" you ask.

The angel replies, "You're pregnant with Jesus. Jesus lives within you through the Holy Spirit. You'll be the dwelling place of Jesus. God is asking you to give birth to Jesus in the ordinary events of your life, to make the presence of Jesus experienced at school, work, home—wherever you are and whomever you're with at the time. You'll carry Jesus within you, just as a pregnant mother carries her baby within her, wherever she goes."

How do the angel's words make you feel? Sit with your feelings. How do you respond to this request? Imagine yourself responding to the angel—what do you say?

OPTIONAL REFLECTION/JOURNAL QUESTIONS

- How do these words impact you: *"Greetings, favored one, the Lord is with you?"*

- What keeps you from fully embracing these words?

- If you could fully receive and embrace these words, how would they impact your view of yourself?

- What does it mean to be "pregnant with Jesus"?

- How would your awareness that you're pregnant with Jesus influence how you interact with others?

[End]

SHEPHERDS IN THE FIELD

Scripture Reference: Luke 2:8-20

Themes: Significance, Joy

SNEAK PEEK

Your students are invited to experience themselves as humble shepherds who are chosen to hear the good news first.

BELLS AND WHISTLES

- Imaginative Prayer Treasure Chest (refer to page 37)

- A manger and the baby Jesus positioned somewhere up front so they're easily visible to everyone

RUNDOWN

1. Slow Down (refer to page 44)

2. Read Imaginative Prayer Meditation.

3. Offer students quiet space for reflection.

4. Optional Reflection/Journal Questions

IMAGINATIVE PRAYER MEDITATION

You're an ordinary, humble shepherd. Several of you are camping in the fields with the sheep, making sure they're safe. The night shift is the worst, so the newest and youngest workers get stuck with it. That's you.

Sitting quietly with two other shepherds around a small campfire, you try to stay alert and listen for sounds of danger. The sky is so dark, you can't see past the light of the fire. Suddenly, someone appears right in front of you—an angel, filled with light. This light completely surrounds you and your friends. It seems to shine straight through you. You scream in terror.

In the midst of your screaming, the angel calls your name and says, "Don't be afraid." You feel your heart calm while you stare at the angel in wonder. "I have the best news to tell you," the angel goes on to say. "Something has happened that will change the whole world. A Savior has been born in Bethlehem. The promised Rescuer is here! You can find the baby wrapped in a blanket and lying in a manger."

As the angel finishes speaking, the entire sky lights up. It's filled with angels as far as you can see! And they begin to sing, "Glory to God, Glory to God! Peace to all women and men!" The music fills the air and seems to fill the entire world. The words are repeated again and again. Over and over you hear, "Glory to God, Glory to God! Peace to all women and men," until the words seep into your bones. Your legs lose their strength and you fall to the ground weeping. Your heart sings with the angels, "Glory to God…!"

Eventually the singing fades, the angels disappear, and the sky turns black again. You slowly pull yourself up from the ground and look around for your friends. You stare at each other wordlessly.

Then you smile. "Let's go find him," you say. You leave the sheep. You leave everything to search for the baby. You find the infant Savior, just as the angel said. You fall to the ground with your heart so full it hurts. You weep while kneeling before this baby, this King, this Promised One.

Then, as you look into the face of Jesus, you smile…and then laugh. You're experiencing a joy you've never known before…and gratitude. How glad you are to be the ordinary shepherd who was chosen to see this baby.

As you and your friends leave, you know you've been changed forever. Dancing, skipping, and singing, you tell everyone you meet what happened. You tell everyone what you saw and heard. Your heart continues to sing the song of the angels, "Glory to God, Glory to God! Peace to all women and men!"

OPTIONAL REFLECTION/JOURNAL QUESTIONS

- Imaginatively return to the manger. You're invited to hold the baby Jesus. Look into baby Jesus' face. What do you see? How do you feel?

- As you rock him gently, consider that Jesus holds you gently as well. You are God's cherished child. How does that feel for you?

- God chooses ordinary people like the shepherds to be a part of God's amazing story. Do you feel chosen as well? Why or why not?

[End]

CHAPTER 10

GOSPEL TIME [FIFTEEN EXERCISES]

NAMES (IMAGES) OF JESUS

Scripture References: Various Scripture Passages

Theme: Images of Jesus

SNEAK PEEK

This exercise helps students focus on a name or image used to describe Jesus and spend some time sitting with it and unpacking it for themselves.

BELLS AND WHISTLES

- Imaginative Prayer Treasure Chest (refer to page 37)

- A variety of supplies—paper, pens, crayons, markers, and clay—to help students explore an image or images of Jesus.

RUNDOWN

1. Slow Down (refer to page 44)

2. After the Slow Down, slowly read through the list of names or images three times.

3. Remind the students to choose a name or title or image of Jesus that is meaningful to them and then use their imagination to reflect on it. For example, *Imagine Jesus as a door. What is a door? What is its purpose? What color door would he be? Or—Imagine Jesus as the Bread of Life. What is bread? What kind of bread would Jesus be? Of what value is bread to the body?*

4. After you've read through the list for the third time, direct the students to an individual time of reflection using the materials you've put together (art and writing supplies, as well as Optional Reflection/Journal Questions to consider).

5. Offer students quiet space for reflection.

6. This is an excellent exercise to debrief as a group. It helps the leader to see what aspects of Jesus the students are attracted to. Plus, as the various names, titles, or images of Jesus are shared, the richness can help to deepen and expand the students' internal sense of who Jesus is.

IMAGINATIVE PRAYER MEDITATION

I'm going to read through a list that contains names or titles or images of Jesus found in the Bible. I'll be reading through this list three times. I want you to listen for a name or title or image of Jesus that makes an impact on you. It can mean something positive or negative—that part doesn't matter.

Then begin to spend time with the image or name of Jesus you've chosen. I want you to use your imagination to reveal its meaning for you, and I've brought a variety of materials to help you explore the name or image of Jesus you've chosen.

NAMES OR TITLES OF JESUS
(Slowly read through the following list of names three times, pausing for a few moments each time you reach the end of the list. Don't read the Scripture references.)

Star (Numbers 24:17); Bright Morning Star (Revelation 22:16)

Immanuel, God with Us (Isaiah 7:14; Matthew 1:23)

Wonderful Counselor (Isaiah 9:6)

Mighty God (Isaiah 9:6)

Prince of Peace (Isaiah 9:6)

Ancient of Days (Daniel 7:9)

King (Zechariah 9:9)

Friend (Matthew 11:19; John 15:13-14)

Servant (Matthew 12:18)

Holy One of God (Mark 1:24)

The Christ (the Messiah, the Anointed One) (Mark 8:29, AMP)

Dayspring or Rising Sun (Luke 1:78, KJV)

The Word (John 1:1; Revelation 19:13)

Lamb of God (John 1:29)

Savior (John 4:42)

Bread of Life (John 6:35)

Light of the World (John 8:12)

I Am (John 8:58)

The Door (John 10:9, KJV)

Good Shepherd (John 10:11)

The Resurrection and the Life (John 11:25)

The Way (John 14:6)

The Truth (John 14:6)

The Life (John 14:6)

The True Vine (John 15:1)

Lord and God (John 20:28)

Rock (1 Corinthians 10:4)

Indescribable Gift (2 Corinthians 9:15)

Alpha and Omega (Revelation 22:13)

OPTIONAL REFLECTION/JOURNAL QUESTIONS

With the image(s) or name(s) of Jesus you've chosen in mind, answer the following questions:

- What does this really mean to me?

- What does this tell me about Jesus?

- How could this help me to love and trust Jesus?

- How does this make me feel toward Jesus?

- How could this help me to live more freely?

(Write these prompting questions on a white board or place them on a handout so the students can see them.)

[End]

GOD WITH US

Scripture References: Matthew 1:23; 28:20; Hebrews 13:5

Theme: Presence of God

SNEAK PEEK

In this exercise the students are asked to walk through a typical day (but with Jesus), starting with when they wake up in the morning and concluding when they go to bed at night.

BELLS AND WHISTLES

- Imaginative Prayer Treasure Chest (refer to page 37)

- As a great aid for this exercise, have the students briefly write about one of their "normal days." Provide students with a piece of paper with one-hour time periods already written on it (e.g., 6-7 a.m., 7-8 a.m., 10-11 p.m., and so on), along with enough space for them to write a brief description of what takes place during each time period of a typical day.

RUNDOWN

1. If you have prepared an hourly calendar for your students to fill out, pass that out now. If not, you may wish to pass out blank paper. Pass out pens.

2. Read Imaginative Prayer Meditation, leading your students through a Slow Down where indicated.

3. Offer students quiet space for reflection. (At this point you may wish to make available the *Optional Reflection/Journal Questions.*

4. After time for individual reflection, you may want to gather the students back together for a group debriefing. Process what it was like to imagine Jesus being present during each part of the day.

IMAGINATIVE PRAYER MEDITATION

Before we begin our exercise, I want each of you to mentally construct a normal day in your life. Begin with getting out of bed in the morning; then proceed through a typical day—school, lunch, hanging out with friends, work, sports, movies, video games, and so on. Your day concludes whenever you crawl into bed at night.

To help you do this, I'm passing out a piece of paper that lists different times of the day. Next to each time slot, write down whatever activity you do during that time, such as get out of bed, eat breakfast, go to school, work, and so on.

(When students are finished writing, read aloud Matthew 1:23; Matthew 28:20; and Hebrews 13:5.) These verses remind us that Jesus is always with us—no matter what. Jesus is with us every moment of the day.

What we're going to do now is have you imagine that Jesus is walking with you throughout the day you've just created. Starting with when you get out of bed, imagine Jesus is with you. He can either be doing the things you're doing, or maybe he's just standing or sitting near you. I want you to slowly process through the activities of each hour you've listed on your sheet, imagining Jesus is right there with you. I've also provided some questions to help you do this.

But first, let's quiet our minds and prepare ourselves for a day spent with Jesus. **(Lead your students through the Slow Down exercise, on page 44, before continuing.)** Now imagine it's just you and Jesus walking through your day together.

OPTIONAL REFLECTION/JOURNAL QUESTIONS

- How did you imagine Jesus felt as he went through your day with you?

- What difference does it make having Jesus with you in terms of how you feel about yourself, the things you do, and the way you treat and feel about others?

- How did the realization that Jesus was with you throughout your day change you, change your day?

- What surprised you?

- What made you uncomfortable?

- Can you share a time when knowing Jesus was with you impacted how you felt, reacted, made a certain choice?

- What makes it hard to remember that Jesus is always with us?

[End]

THE LORD'S PRAYER

Scripture References: Matthew 6:9-15; Luke 5:16

Theme: Prayer

SNEAK PEEK

Students will be guided into an encounter with Jesus involving the Lord's Prayer.

BELLS AND WHISTLES

- Imaginative Prayer Treasure Chest (refer to page 37)

RUNDOWN

1. Slow Down (refer to page 44)

2. Read Imaginative Prayer Meditation.

3. At the end of the exercise, you'll say the Lord's Prayer and have the students repeat after you. Go through the prayer slowly, and don't be afraid to change the words so they're more fitting for your students. Let the students have some time to reflect on the words by breaking it up into smaller pieces: Our Father…who lives in heaven…special is your name…

4. Offer students quiet space for reflection.

5. Optional Reflection/Journal Questions

IMAGINATIVE PRAYER MEDITATION

You've spent the night sleeping in the same room as Jesus and the disciples. Now it's early in the morning. The sun isn't up yet, the air is cold, and you turn over to get some more sleep. You pull the covers up around your neck. You feel warm and cozy. As you're about to drift back to sleep, you hear someone get up. This person leaves the room and heads toward the front door. You decide to follow and see what's going on.

You now realize that you're following Jesus. Is he on his way to meet someone, do a miracle, or have it out with the Pharisees? You don't want to miss out, so you grab your sandals, wrap yourself in a blanket, and head out the front door behind him.

You walk quickly at first, closing the space between you and Jesus, but not so close that Jesus can see you. You'll move closer once Jesus begins to do whatever it is he's planning to do. You feel your heart racing. Not because you're walking so fast, but because you sense that Jesus is up to something big. You think about some of his recent miracles—healing the leper and the blind man and the paralyzed man, bringing a child back to life, multiplying the bread.

You and Jesus have been walking down a dirt path, but now he cuts through a meadow and heads toward a hill covered with olive trees. You continue to follow him. When Jesus reaches the bottom of the hill, he begins to climb. There are a great number of trees, and you soon lose sight of him. You enter the trees where you think he might be, but you're unable to find him. So you stop walking and just listen—for the crunching of leaves, the breaking of a twig that might indicate where Jesus is. You hear nothing.

You feel a little disappointed but decide to keep moving forward. You continue to walk slowly up the hill while trying to be very quiet, hoping you'll hear something that will help you figure out where Jesus is. Again you hear nothing. You're almost ready to go back when you see someone out of the corner of your eye. You move closer and discover it's Jesus sitting in a clearing among the trees.

You hear him talking. You slowly move closer and use the trees to block his view of you. When Jesus stops speaking, there is silence. You freeze. You don't want him to know you're there. You strain to hear the other person's voice, but you still can't hear anything.

After a long period of silence, you finally hear a voice. But it's just Jesus speaking again. You can't make out his words. Who is he talking to? What is he talking about? You begin to inch ever closer, moving as quietly as possible.

After Jesus finishes talking once more, there is another long period of silence. What's going on? You move even closer and as you do, you step on a small branch. CRACK! The tiny sound seems to echo loudly through the silent trees and off down the hill. Now Jesus turns toward you. You feel embarrassed, but he motions you over.

So you walk toward him. Jesus seems happy to see you, happy you're there. As you get to Jesus, you realize there's no one else around. Did the other person run away when you stepped on that branch? Did you mess up Jesus' plan?

Jesus, seemingly knowing your thoughts, says, "I'm glad you're here. Don't worry, there was no one else here. I was praying. Would you like to pray with me?" You nod "yes" and Jesus smiles. He says, "I'll teach you a special prayer. I'll say it first, and you repeat after me."

(Now read aloud the Lord's Prayer from Matthew 6:9-13. Below is how it's found in the New International Version, but you may wish to read it from a different translation.)

Our Father in heaven,

hallowed be your name,

your kingdom come,

your will be done

on earth as it is in heaven.

Give us today our daily bread.

Forgive us our debts,

as we also have forgiven our debtors.

And lead us not into temptation,

but deliver us from the evil one.

OPTIONAL REFLECTION/JOURNAL QUESTIONS

- Why was prayer so important to Jesus?

- Why does God want you to pray?

- What part does prayer play in your life?

- To whom do you pray? Why?

- How do you think God feels about your prayers?

- What goes on inside you before you pray, while you're praying, and after you pray?

- Is it difficult or easy for you to pray? Why?

- What words from the prayer Jesus taught you are the most meaningful to you? Sit with them.

- What words from the Lord's Prayer are the most difficult for you to pray?

- Why do you think Jesus taught people this prayer?

[End]

"I NEVER KNEW YOU"

Scripture Reference: Matthew 7:21-23

Theme: Being Versus Doing

SNEAK PEEK

This exercise moves right into an individual time of interaction between the student and Jesus. It deals with the whole "being versus doing" aspect of our relationship with God. At the end of the Imaginative Prayer Meditation, the students will write down a question for Jesus and then prayerfully wait for, and then record, Jesus' reply. Continue this process until the students are finished.

BELLS AND WHISTLES

- Imaginative Prayer Treasure Chest (refer to page 37)

- Pens or pencils and paper for each student

RUNDOWN

1. Slow Down (refer to page 44)

2. Read Imaginative Prayer Meditation.

3. Offer students quiet space for reflection.

4. Have students write down their questions and Jesus' replies.

5. Optional Reflection/Journal Questions

IMAGINATIVE PRAYER MEDITATION

You're walking down a country road headed into town. You're alone, and the road is deserted. You walk slowly for you're in no rush, but your mind jumps around from one thought to the next. You hear your sandals slap against your feet as they strike the dry, hard ground. The birds are singing. The leaves in the trees are dancing upon the gentle breeze. You feel the sun on your face. You close your eyes for a moment to drink in the sun's warmth.

You're headed nowhere in particular, just walking toward town without any particular plan for the day. As you near the town, you see a crowd of people gathered outside an old house. They appear to be hanging out and talking among themselves, maybe waiting for someone or for something to happen.

You're curious, so you approach someone and ask, "What's going on?"

The person replies, "We're here to see Jesus. He's inside that house, and we're waiting for him to come out."

You ask, "Why?"

"We're here to tell Jesus what we've been up to. We'll tell him all the things we've done for him—done in his name. You see, we've all done some amazing things." The person looks around the crowd and begins pointing to people and sharing what they've done—each accomplishment more amazing than the last. "That one over there healed the sick; those three have told of future events; that other one gave all his money to the poor; and that one cast out numerous demons in the name of Jesus!" The person goes on and on, telling you all about the incredible deeds these individuals have performed in Jesus' name.

As you look around, you notice these people look just like you—ordinary, nothing special—in fact, you could be one of them. But you haven't done anything that great. Inside you feel badly; you think, *What have I done for Jesus?* These people are no different from you, but they've done these wondrous things in Jesus' name, while sometimes you struggle to remember to pray before you go to bed.

You're momentarily lost to your own thoughts when you faintly hear from the front of the crowd, "There he is! He's coming out to meet us!" You refocus on your present surroundings. You see Jesus walking from the house, down the rock path, through the white gate, and out into the crowd. The people become animated—each person calling out to Jesus and telling him what they've done. They excitedly try to push their way forward to get closer to Jesus. You hear people saying, "Lord, I prophesied in Your name!" "I healed people!" "I gave all my money to the poor!" "Lord, I cast out demons!"

After listening to this go on for a few minutes, Jesus raises his hands to quiet everyone down. There is a brief moment of complete silence. Then a murmur of excitement works its way through the crowd, "Jesus is going to speak! Jesus is going to speak!" Though the people are quiet, you can sense their anticipation as they wait to hear Jesus' words.

Jesus speaks to the crowd in a powerful and firm voice, "Not everyone who says to me, 'Lord, Lord,' will enter the kingdom of heaven, but only he who does the will of my Father who is in heaven. Many will say to me on that day, 'Lord, Lord, did we not prophesy in your name, and in your name drive out demons and perform many miracles?' Then I'll tell them plainly, 'I never knew you. Away from me, you evildoers!'"

You can't believe your ears. You look around and see faces filled with confusion or anger, while still others turn away from Jesus with their heads bowed and their shoulders slumped as they slowly trudge off. You stand there in disbelief. These people had all done incredible things, yet Jesus said to them, "I never knew you, get out of here, you're evil." How could he say such harsh things? This seems wrong.

As you think about all of this, the crowd continues to thin out until only you and Jesus are left. Jesus walks over to you. He calls you by name. "What are you thinking? What are you feeling?" he asks. You share your thoughts with him, telling him how you feel about what he just said and asking him to tell you what he meant.

Listen to Jesus as he responds to you. Continue to ask your questions and listen to Jesus' answers.

OPTIONAL REFLECTION/JOURNAL QUESTIONS

- What feelings about Jesus did this story stir up in you?

- How did you picture Jesus as he spoke to the others in the story? Mad, sad, disappointed, frustrated?

- How did you picture Jesus as he spoke to you? Mad, sad, disappointed, frustrated?

- What is one question you asked Jesus? Why was this question important to you?

- How did Jesus respond to your question?

- What surprised you about Jesus' response to you?

[End]

REST

Scripture Reference: Matthew 11:28-30

Theme: Rest

SNEAK PEEK

We tend to ignore the Sabbath, but rest is a gift of great value. In this exercise your students are encouraged to receive this gift.

BELLS AND WHISTLES

- Imaginative Prayer Treasure Chest (refer to page 37)

- Pillows and blankets

- A beautifully wrapped package

- Be ready to put the word REST on a big screen once the gift is opened.

RUNDOWN

- Slow Down (refer to page 44)

- Read Imaginative Prayer Meditation.

- Offer students quiet space for reflection.

- Optional Reflection/Journal Questions

[End]

IMAGINATIVE PRAYER MEDITATION

You're throwing a party. The place is decorated, food and beverages are being eaten, and people are laughing and enjoying themselves. Watching the room, you smile. It's a good party. Joining in for just a moment, you sit on the couch and listen to a few stories. The couch is comfy, and you realize how tired you are. You've worked hard to put this shindig together. But then you're up again, refilling glasses, answering the door, and hugging old friends.

You hear your name and turn to see God standing in front of you. God is standing there wearing a goofy grin and holding out a gift. You take the beautifully wrapped package and thank him for the unexpected surprise. Setting the present on the table, you ask if there's anything you can get for God—a beverage maybe? Some food? In response, God wonders if you have time to sit on the couch for a bit. But at that moment you notice a friend who's been waiting to talk to you. Her parents are splitting up. So you excuse yourself and walk over to her, listening with compassion as your friend shares her sad story about her family's problems. You really wish you could help her.

Eventually, you wander over toward the food table to check supplies. Once again you see God standing there, holding the same gift out to you. After you thank God and take the gift again, you ask if there's anything God would like. God wonders if you have time to sit on the couch for a bit, but just then another friend interrupts you with some great news about a scholarship. Setting the gift on the table, you listen as he excitedly shares his news.

You're excited for him, knowing how hard he's been working to earn this financial reward.

As you give your friend one last congratulatory hug and turn to walk away, God is standing right behind you. God picks up the gift again and holds it out to you.

"Do you want me to open it now?" you ask. God's head bobs up and down in obvious excitement about the gift. You begin to feel excited, too. What could it be? It's from God after all, so it's probably pretty great.

You find a place to sit on the couch, and God sits down, too. God is nearly giggly at the thought of you opening your gift. You suddenly realize it must be a big deal. It must be really wonderful. You smile at God, stifle a tired yawn, and then look at your gift, feeling even more excited. It's beautifully wrapped in blue, green, and gold paper with a large gold ribbon tied around it. It's shiny and sparkly. You hate to rip it open, but God's about to do it for you, so you go ahead.

The paper's all torn off now, and you begin to lift the lid off the box. Inside, nestled among crinkled sheets of sparkly gold tissue paper, you see a single word: REST. **(At this point, project the word REST on a large screen.)** You look up at God and then back to the gift. REST. God's face is childlike and filled with sheer excitement, but you're confused. What do you do with this? God is now smiling and nodding, wordlessly encouraging you to take out your gift. Reaching down into the box, you pick up REST and hold it in your hands. Suddenly, the room falls silent.

You look around to see that you and God are now alone. The party is over, the room is clean, and the couch is still comfy. You smile. Putting an arm around you, God smiles. You lay your head on the shoulder of God, the One who invites you to rest. Letting out a sigh, you close your eyes and say, "Thank you."

OPTIONAL REFLECTION/JOURNAL QUESTIONS

- How did you feel when you found out what the gift was? Can you name your emotions?

- Do you allow yourself to rest—especially in God's arms—and simply stop working, worrying, or figuring things out? Why or why not?

- Would you like to rest in God's arms now? Talk to God about that.

[End]

"WHO DO YOU SAY I AM?" (JESUS)

Scripture Reference: Matthew 16:13-16

Theme: Images of Jesus

SNEAK PEEK

The student is asked by Jesus, "Who do you say I am?" This is an excellent exercise to lead into a time of talking about who Jesus is and who Jesus declared himself to be.

BELLS AND WHISTLES

- Imaginative Prayer Treasure Chest (refer to page 37)

- You may wish to have the titles of Jesus on pages 94-95 typed on a handout so you can distribute them to the students during the debriefing time.

RUNDOWN

1. Slow Down (refer to page 44)

2. Read Imaginative Prayer Meditation.

3. Offer students quiet space for reflection.

4. Optional Reflection/Journal Questions

IMAGINATIVE PRAYER MEDITATION

You're standing with the disciples, just hanging around and not really doing much of anything. Jesus comes over and asks all of you a question, "Who do you say I am?" Before you can even think of an answer, Peter blurts out, "You are the Christ, the Son of the living God." Then the question is dropped.

But you can't get the question out of your mind. You keep thinking about how *you* would have answered Jesus. Who is Jesus to you? Take some time and formulate your answer(s) to this question. Try and get past the churchy answers and listen to your heart, deep down, deep within you—who do you say Jesus is?

When you're ready with your answer, imagine Jesus asking you, "Who do you say I am?" **(Pause a moment.)**

Give your response to Jesus. Notice how you feel as you share your answer with him. Notice how he reacts to your answer. Notice how you feel as Jesus responds to your answer. **(Allow significant pause.)**

Now turn to Jesus and ask him, "Who do you say you are?" Listen as I read a list of Jesus' descriptions of himself. Notice the descriptions you're drawn to. Notice the ones that are missing from your description of Jesus. **(Don't read aloud the Scripture references that follow each statement.)**

I am Immanuel—God with you. (Isaiah 7:14; Matthew 1:23)

I am the Wonderful Counselor. (Isaiah 9:6)

I am the Mighty God. (Isaiah 9:6)

I am the Prince of Peace. (Isaiah 9:6)

I am the One who was beaten and pierced through in your place because of love. (Isaiah 53:5)

I am the King. (Zechariah 9:9)

I am your faithful friend. (Matthew 11:19)

I am God's servant. (Matthew 12:18)

I am the Holy One of God. (Mark 1:24)

I am the Great Healer. (Mark 3:1-12)

I am the Christ—the Anointed One—the Messiah—the Savior of the world. (Mark 8:29, AMP)

I am God clothed in flesh. (Luke 2:8-20)

I am kind and merciful. (Luke 6:35-36)

I am compassionate. (Luke 6:35-36)

I am the living Word of God. (John 1:1,14; Revelation 19:13)

I am the Creator. (John 1:2-4)

I am the Lamb of God. (John 1:29)

I am the One who would rather suffer and die for you than live without you. (John 3:16)

I am the Bread of Life. (John 6:35)

I am the Giver of life everlasting. (John 6:40, 47)

I am the Light of the World. (John 8:12)

I am God. (John 8:58; 10:30; 20:28)

I am the Door to God. (John 10:9, KJV)

I am the Good Shepherd. (John 10:11)

I am the One who lays down his life for those I love. (John 10:11)

I am the Resurrection and the Life. (John 11:25)

I am the Way to God. (John 14:6)

I am the Truth. (John 14:6)

I am the Life of God. (John 14:6)

I am the True Vine. (John 15:1)

I am he who died on the cross and rose from the dead. (John 19–20)

I am the Rock upon which you can build your life. (1 Corinthians 10:4)

I am the One before whom every knee will bow and tongue confess that I am Lord. (Philippians 2:9-11)

I am the One who will never leave you nor forsake you. (Hebrews 13:5)

I am the Beginning and the End. (Revelation 22:13)

OPTIONAL REFLECTION/JOURNAL QUESTIONS

- How did you feel as you shared your answer with Jesus?

- How did Jesus react to your answer?

- How did you feel as Jesus responded to your answer?

- What would you now add to your original answer concerning who Jesus is?

- Which descriptions are you drawn to and which ones were missing from your description of Jesus? Why?

- What qualities do your chosen descriptions of Jesus reflect (his love, power, grace, mercy…)?

- Why are those qualities important to you?

[End]

"WHO DO YOU SAY I AM?" (US)

Scripture Reference: Matthew 16:13-16

Theme: Identity

SNEAK PEEK

In this exercise the students will reflect on who the Bible declares *them* to be. They're asked to choose one of the statements and spend time reflecting on it.

BELLS AND WHISTLES

- Imaginative Prayer Treasure Chest (refer to page 37)

- Ahead of time, you may wish to prepare and photocopy the list of terms that describe who Jesus says we are (pages 97-98) for the students to refer to during the debriefing. Or project them onto a screen for all to see.

RUNDOWN

1. Slow Down (refer to page 44)

2. Read Imaginative Prayer Meditation.

3. Offer students quiet space for reflection.

4. Optional Reflection/Journal Questions

IMAGINATIVE PRAYER MEDITATION

You are heading down the road from Jerusalem to Galilee with Jesus and the disciples. You'll walk nearly all day to get to Galilee. Peter is leading the way, as usual, and the rest of you are bunched together. You're just walking and talking. There's no rush, nothing to do. And Jesus is a little way behind the group, walking by himself. You decide to drop back and walk with him for a while. You slow your pace a little and soon you and Jesus are walking side-by-side. You walk in silence for several minutes. There is much you want to say but there are no words.

Jesus finally breaks the silence. He calls you by name and asks what's on your mind. Your mind goes blank, and you stare back helplessly; no words will form in your mind or on your lips. Jesus waits and then asks you again, "Would you like to talk about something?" You remember a prior conversation

between Jesus and the disciples when Jesus asked them, *Who do you say I am?* You decide to ask that very question of Jesus.

Even though it seems to be a strange question, you say to Jesus, "Jesus, who do you say I am?"

Jesus immediately smiles and chuckles a bit before saying, "That is an excellent question. I'll answer you; but before I do, I want you to sit down, close your eyes, and listen very closely and carefully to my answer."

(Each time you read through the following list, begin by reading this next paragraph.) "All that I'm about to say to you is true. I want you to pay special attention to the words I use to describe you—the ones you really like, as well as those you have trouble believing. Remember—every word I say will be true of you. Now sit down, close your eyes, and listen with your heart, as well as with your mind and your ears."

You are chosen and dearly loved by God.

You are the salt of the earth.

You are the light of the world.

You are God's child, prized and treasured by God.

You are my friend.

You are a saint.

You are forgiven—past, present, and future.

You are and always will be an object of God's love—an object of my love.

You are a citizen of heaven.

You are the temple of God—God dwells within you.

You are a new creation (new person).

You are God's coworker.

You are an heir of God.

You are God's workmanship—a masterpiece, unique in all the world.

You are righteous and holy—in you there is no flaw.

You are the chosen one of God.

You are holy.

You are dearly and uniquely loved by God.

You are a chosen race.

You are a royal priesthood.

You belong to God and God belongs to you.

You are one who will always be with me.

You are a source of delight to God.

OPTIONAL REFLECTION/JOURNAL QUESTIONS

- What do the words of Jesus communicate to you about how Jesus sees you?

- How do these words make you feel? What about them makes you feel that way?

- How does Jesus feel about you?

- How does Jesus want you to feel about yourself?

- Which descriptions mean the most to you? Why?

- Is it easy or difficult to believe that these wonderful things Jesus said are true about you? Why?

- Which are the hardest ones for you to believe about yourself?

[End]

COMING TO JESUS

Scripture References: Mark 10:13-16; Luke 18:15-17

Themes: Desire, Trust, Loneliness

SNEAK PEEK

This exercise invites the listener to be a child who desires to approach Jesus. Your students are invited to consider whether or not they wish to approach Jesus and then ponder some things that may deter them.

BELLS AND WHISTLES

- Imaginative Prayer Treasure Chest (refer to page 37)

- Image of child appearing hesitant, unsure, or perhaps sad.

RUNDOWN

1. Slow Down (refer to page 44)

2. Read Imaginative Prayer Meditation.

3. Offer students quiet space for reflection.

4. Optional Reflection/Journal Questions

IMAGINATIVE PRAYER MEDITATION

It's late afternoon. You're a young child standing off to the side of a large group of grown-ups. It's hot and dusty; the sun is beating down on your face. You've been here for hours. There are no other children nearby, and you feel alone.

There's an ache inside you, a need to be seen and held and loved. It's been there a long time, and it's the reason you can't seem to leave. That lonely pain deep inside you lessens as you watch the man in the middle of the crowd. You can't stop looking at him and listening to his voice. It's deep and gentle, and his eyes are kind. Jesus is his name.

You wish you could be near him, but the crowd is big and you're awfully little. Maybe you could squeeze through the people and get closer to Jesus. Maybe you could touch his face and sit on his lap. What a crazy idea! There are so many people here, and they *all* want Jesus' attention. He's busy with important things, and giving you a hug doesn't feel very important—except it is to you.

The day is almost over, and you need to make a decision. Maybe you should just go home. Maybe you can see Jesus another day, when there are fewer people around. Or you can try to move forward and ask Jesus to provide what you want and need, risking rejection, embarrassment, and failure.

OPTIONAL REFLECTION/JOURNAL QUESTIONS

- As you imaginatively stand alone and apart from the crowd, what emotions come up for you? See if you can name them.

- What decision do you make? Do you go home or do you move toward Jesus?

- Why do you think you made that decision?

- How do you think Jesus feels about your decision? Why?

- How does Jesus respond to your choice? Notice his expression, what he might say, what he might do.

[End]

WOMAN WITH THE ALABASTER JAR

Scripture Reference: Mark 14:3-9

Themes: Desire, Courage, Loved by God

SNEAK PEEK

Your students are invited to enter a dinner party and observe as a woman boldly approaches Jesus without any thought of what others may think of her actions. They're also invited to consider their own issues regarding what people think of them.

BELLS AND WHISTLES

- Imaginative Prayer Treasure Chest (refer to page 37)
- Big, beautiful perfume bottle

RUNDOWN

1. Slow Down (refer to page 44)

2. Read Imaginative Prayer Meditation.

3. Offer students quiet space for reflection.

4. Optional Reflection/Journal Questions

IMAGINATIVE PRAYER MEDITATION

The scene is a house in Bethany. Jesus is present. The house is full of people. You're standing against a wall near the door, watching everything that's taking place.

You notice a woman enter the room. She hesitates, but only for a moment. You see fear in her eyes. But there's also something else in her expression—determination. She stands near the door and scans the room until she sees Jesus. Her eyes soften and the fear seems to evaporate instantly.

You watch as she walks over to Jesus. She doesn't say a word, but tears stream down her face. Yet she doesn't wipe them away. Maybe she doesn't notice them. Stopping next to Jesus as he reclines at the table, she pulls out a beautiful alabaster jar. She breaks it open and an amazing fragrance fills the room. Then she begins pouring the contents on Jesus' head.

The room has grown silent, and everyone is now staring at her. She either doesn't notice or doesn't care.

People begin murmuring to each other, complaining. They don't like having her at this party. They don't approve of her and don't like what she's doing. They say she's wasted a lot of good perfume on Jesus—more than a year's wages worth! Now they're asking her to leave Jesus alone and go away.

The woman's tear-filled eyes look only at Jesus. She's smiling at him, and her face is a picture of peace. How can that be? Everyone is looking at her and speaking to her so harshly. No one thinks she belongs here.

Well, no one except Jesus. He smiles and looks at her with love and gentleness. He speaks to the people sitting around him and firmly tells *them* to leave *her* alone. He looks into her eyes as he tells the others that she has done a beautiful thing for him. He bends low and speaks quietly to the woman.

Look at Jesus' eyes and realize why this woman isn't afraid. Who could be afraid when eyes of love look into your soul? What if those eyes looked at you that way, too? Would you become bold and unafraid, not caring what anyone else thinks? Do you want him to look at you? Do you want to be the one Jesus sees, the one Jesus defends, the one Jesus intimately speaks with?

Suddenly, Jesus turns his head toward you. His eyes seem to look inside of you with love and delight; he smiles. How do you respond? Do you return his gaze? **(Pause a moment.)** Now he's motioning you over to him. You're invited to spend time with Jesus, not caring what anyone else might think. Respond with your heart, noticing if you want to approach him or not. Say, do, and be whoever you truly are in front of Jesus.

OPTIONAL REFLECTION/JOURNAL QUESTIONS

- What did you experience as you watched the woman courageously enter the dinner party and express her love to Jesus?

- What did you feel as people started to complain about the woman and what she was doing? Why?

- What did you experience as you watched her interact with Jesus? And as Jesus defended her?

- When Jesus looks at you, are you drawn to him? Why or why not? Do you choose to join him?

- How do you think Jesus feels about your choice? Why?

- How does Jesus respond to your choice? Notice his expression, what he might say, what he might do.

[End]

GOOD SAMARITAN

Scripture Reference: Luke 10:30-37

Theme: Loving Others

SNEAK PEEK

This exercise uses a current-day scene inspired by the question, *Who is my neighbor?*

BELLS AND WHISTLES

- Imaginative Prayer Treasure Chest (refer to page 37)

RUNDOWN

1. Slow Down (refer to page 44)

2. Read Imaginative Prayer Meditation.

3. Offer students quiet space for reflection.

4. Optional Reflection/Journal Questions

IMAGINATIVE PRAYER MEDITATION

It's Saturday morning, and you're running late. You quickly check your backpack one more time to see if you've forgotten anything. You have your books, paper, pencils, and some cash. Guess that's it. You're off to meet a few friends to study for your history final on Monday, and then you're all going out for pizza and a movie.

You hate to spend a perfectly good Saturday studying for a test, but it helps that you get to go out afterward. And you're happy to be spending the day with your good friends. You're a tight group, but lately you've been unable to get together as much as you used to. So this is a great opportunity and you're happy to have it—even if it includes studying!

As you turn the corner, the new neighbor kid catches up with you. He wants to know where you're going. He wonders if you're ready for that history final because he's not. Would you like to study together? He doesn't have any plans today. He'd love to hang out with you. He seems to be talking nonstop. You know he's lonely and just trying to make friends, but he's really trying too hard.

Take a moment to consider your response to this neighbor. What feelings come up for you when you look at him and while he's talking to you? What do you do? Ask God to help you find the answer to these questions—not the "church answer" but the answer in your own heart.

OPTIONAL REFLECTION/JOURNAL QUESTIONS

- Do you know people like this new neighbor?

- How does your heart respond to them?

- Do you sometimes feel like the new neighbor yourself? If yes, what feelings came up for you?

- You're invited to process your thoughts and feelings with God.

[End]

MARTHA

Scripture Reference: Luke 10:38-42

Themes: Loved by God, Significance

SNEAK PEEK

Martha longs to please Jesus, but she finds herself feeling frustrated and overlooked. Jesus invites her to be who she's created to be and to follow her heart. Your students are invited to do the same.

BELLS AND WHISTLES

- Imaginative Prayer Treasure Chest (refer to page 37)

- A chair with cushions scattered on the floor all around it

RUNDOWN

1. Slow Down (refer to page 44)

2. Read Imaginative Prayer Meditation.

3. Offer students quiet space for reflection.

4. Optional Reflection/Journal Questions

IMAGINATIVE PRAYER MEDITATION

Jesus is coming! Your heart is beating fast. You've been waiting for him to arrive, and now you see him walking up the road toward your home. But there's still so much to do! Dinner is not prepared, and your sister, Mary, hasn't finished cleaning up the living room yet.

When you see Jesus coming closer, you start to panic. Oh no, oh no. Everything isn't perfect yet. You must work quickly! The door slams, and you jerk your head around. Mary is gone! And she's left you with everything to finish so she can run off to meet Jesus on the road. Ah! She's so irresponsible and selfish!

You turn back toward your chores, and with a determined look you start working again. You'll deal with Mary later. You must concentrate on things other than your lazy sister because you want Jesus to be pleased with all that you've prepared for his visit.

When you hear the door open again, you rush out of the kitchen and greet Jesus. You fluff the pillows and try to lead Jesus to the most comfortable spot in the room. Instead, he stops and grabs your hand. You look up at him and he smiles. You give him a quick, distracted smile, then pull away. "There's more work to do in the kitchen," you explain and then excuse yourself.

Surely Mary will follow me, you think. But she doesn't. Why is it that you're working feverishly, while Mary just sits around? Doesn't Jesus see how hard you're working? Doesn't he see how lazy and irresponsible Mary is being?

That's it. You've had enough. You walk into the living room and confront Jesus. "Lord, don't you care that my sister has left me to do the work by myself? Tell her to help me!" Jesus looks right into your eyes and says, "Martha, Martha, you are worried and upset about many things, but only a few things are important—actually only one. Mary has chosen to follow her heart."

Jesus stands. He takes your hands in his and says, "There's nothing you need to do to please me. I am already pleased with you. Just as you are." Then he asks, "If you followed your heart, what would you do right now? It's okay if you choose differently than Mary, and it's okay if you choose to do the same. Listen to your own heart and follow it."

Where does your heart lead you? Spend some time pondering Jesus' question. Do you head back to the kitchen where you can work with your hands and prepare something wonderful for Jesus to eat? Or do you join Mary on the floor at Jesus' feet? You already please Jesus just because you're you. So what do you really want to do?

OPTIONAL REFLECTION/JOURNAL QUESTIONS

- Where do you end up? In the kitchen or at Jesus' feet? Or do you need to leave the house altogether? What's going on inside of you?

- Do you want to tell Jesus what's on your own heart? You're invited to do so now.

- Do you ever feel as though you need to please Jesus?

- How does it feel to be given the freedom (by Jesus) to choose whether you'll serve or sit and listen?

- Which (serving or sitting and listening) is more difficult for you to do? Why?

[End]

THE PRODIGAL

Scripture Reference: Luke 15:11-24

Themes: Forgiveness, Acceptance, Grace

SNEAK PEEK

The students will be asked to imagine they're the child who leaves home with a bad attitude and some hateful words, then later decides to return home.

BELLS AND WHISTLES

- Imaginative Prayer Treasure Chest (refer to page 37)

- Projection or large poster of Rembrandt's "The Return of the Prodigal Son." It would also be great if you could order some postcard-sized individual prints of this painting for each of your students to have. You can order a very nice poster and postcards (called "meditation cards") from www.henrinouwen.org. (The poster costs about $20, and the cards cost around 75 cents each.)

RUNDOWN

1. Slow Down (refer to page 44)

2. Read Imaginative Prayer Meditation.

3. Offer students quiet space for reflection.

4. Optional Reflection/Journal Questions

IMAGINATIVE PRAYER MEDITATION

It's morning. You wake up in a very bad mood. You're disgusted with your life and your family—you've had enough. You just want what is yours. You also want the freedom to make your own decisions for a change, to live life the way *you* want to live it. You've wanted this long enough—today is the day.

You march into your dad's room and demand what is yours. The angry words flow from your mouth, tinged with hatred, "Dad, I wish you were dead; and I want what is mine—now. Give me my inheritance." Your dad doesn't react in anger, he merely says "okay." He walks to his desk, scribbles out some numbers on a sheet of paper, then moves to the safe and takes out sacks full of money. You can't believe your eyes. He's doing it. He's giving you your inheritance!

Your dad says, "Here you go."

Wow—so much money, and it's all *your* money to do with however you please. You grab it and head out the door. You're in too much of a hurry to see the love in your dad's eyes, to hear the pain in his voice as he whispers good-bye and wishes you the best of luck.

You're free! Free to live however you want and free to make your own decisions. As you walk away from the only home you've ever known, you imagine the fun you'll have and the fortune you'll make for yourself. But soon enough, you get caught up in a lifestyle of parties, drugs, and all that goes along with those kinds of things. You're surrounded by many people who claim to be your friends. That is, until your money runs out. And it disappears pretty quickly, just like your "friends."

Now you're alone and hungry with no place to stay. So you get a job feeding pigs. Your hopes and dreams now mock you, as does your last encounter with your dad. You're so hungry; you're tempted to eat some of the pigs' food. *This is not good*, you think to yourself. *No one should have to live this way.* But what can you do? You remember your dad and think back to the harsh words you said to him before you left home. *I can't go back there, no way!* But what other choice do you have?

You wonder if your dad would be willing to hire you as a servant—at least then you'd get three meals a day and have a roof over your head. You decide to give it a try. You'll go back home, throw yourself on the mercy of your father, and beg him to let you be his servant.

As you begin your journey home, you try to convince yourself that your dad will take you back. You rehearse the scene in your head. *What should I say and how will I say it?* You come up with a plan. You'll fall at his feet and say, "Dad, I was wrong. I messed up, I blew it, and I don't deserve to be your child. I wasted everything you gave to me. Please hire me as your servant. I'll work hard and pay back every last dime."

You practice your speech over and over while imagining your father's stern look and his harsh words, which only reinforce how much you've hurt and dishonored your dad, your family, and yourself; how you've let down your father and everyone else; and how it's not fair to your older brother for you to just come back like nothing happened.

But then you imagine your dad agreeing to let you work as a servant, allowing you to work and sleep in the servants' quarters, but wanting nothing else to do with you. You can hear your dad saying, "I'm only doing this so you can pay back all the money you wasted." Over and over you play out this scene in your mind. **(Pause a moment.)**

Finally, you get close enough to see your home, just as the sun is setting. You see someone standing at the front gate. The figure begins running toward you, and as it gets closer, you can see it's your dad. Your dad is running! You've never seen your dad run before. What can this mean?

As your dad gets closer, you see tears streaming down his face. When he finally reaches you, he throws his arms around you and begins to kiss you. You try to drop to your knees so you can begin begging for a job, but your dad is holding you so tightly you can't do it. Instead, you begin reciting your speech; but your dad isn't listening. He's giving orders to the servants who followed him from the house.

You hear your father's words. They seem strange. They're not filled with judgment, anger, or disappointment, but with love and joy. This isn't how you pictured the scene at all. Your father finishes instructing the servants and they go running off. But in a few minutes, they return with a beautiful robe, fine shoes, and the family ring. Your father gently places the ring on your finger and says, "We're going to have a feast! We're going to celebrate because my precious child has returned home! It's time for music and celebration. My child was lost but now my child has returned. My child was dead but now is alive. Let the party begin!"

OPTIONAL REFLECTION/JOURNAL QUESTIONS

- Have you ever run away from God? Why or why not?

- What were the circumstances that caused you to want to run away from God?

- What does this story tell you about God's love for you?

- How does God's love for you make you feel?

- What surprises you about this story?

- How does this story make you feel about God? About yourself?

[End]

JOHN'S DISCIPLE FOLLOWS JESUS

Scripture Reference: John 1:29-39

Theme: Desire

SNEAK PEEK

Jesus will ask your students, "What do you want?" It's important that you let them sit with this question before they answer it.

BELLS AND WHISTLES

- Imaginative Prayer Treasure Chest (refer to page 37)

RUNDOWN

1. Slow Down (refer to page 44)

2. Read Imaginative Prayer Meditation.

3. Offer students quiet space for reflection.

4. Optional Reflection/Journal Questions

IMAGINATIVE PRAYER MEDITATION

You've been following John the Baptist for a number of months. You like him. He tells it like it is. He isn't afraid of those in power. His message is simple and powerful, calling people to admit their sins and be baptized. His fame is spreading and many believe he's the Promised One, the Messiah, the One the writers of the Old Testament spoke about who would come to bring freedom to the nation of Israel. John has denied this and instead speaks of another who would follow him, one who would be greater—far greater—than John the Baptist would ever be.

One day you're standing with John on a corner in the city. People are moving up and down the street. Some stop and talk to John, asking religious-type questions; others share with John what God has been doing in their lives. The city is alive with people. Children are running here and there. Many folks pause to look at John, a big man dressed in camel hair with a long, bushy beard.

John is now in conversation with a shopkeeper. You're watching the two men talk when John glances up the street and begins to stare at a man walking toward you. You watch John's eyes widen and you hear him say, "Look, the Lamb of God that takes away the sin of the world! This is the One I've been telling you about, the One who is going to come after me."

You've been with John the Baptist for a number of months; but should you follow this other person now? You wonder, *What should I do?* As you're thinking this through, the person John was referring to disappears into the crowd.

The words of John stay with you, "The Lamb of God that takes away the sin of the world! This is the One who is going to come after me." You can't get John's words out of your mind. Your heart feels troubled but you don't know why. The next day you and John the Baptist are in town when the same man appears. Again, John announces, "Look, the Lamb of God!" Yesterday you wondered what John was saying and why. Today, you decide to follow this person, this one they call Jesus. You wonder if John is right—is he truly the One spoken of by the prophets, sent by God to us, the One who will bring freedom and peace?

Now you're walking behind Jesus, matching him step for step. What will this Jesus be like? What does John mean when he says Jesus is far greater than he is and that Jesus baptizes in the Spirit and not merely with water? What does it mean that Jesus is the Lamb of God who takes away the sin of the world? These and other questions dance around in your head. You continue walking behind Jesus, but you're lost in your thoughts.

Taking a quick look to see where Jesus is, you see he's stopped and is standing three feet away—looking right at you. You freeze and feel awkward and unsure that following Jesus was ever a good idea. Jesus looks you in the eye and asks you, "What do you want? What do you most deeply desire?" Jesus waits patiently for your answer. What do you most truly and deeply desire? **(Allow significant pause.)**

OPTIONAL REFLECTION/JOURNAL QUESTIONS

- How did you feel when Jesus asked you what you wanted?

- Were you surprised by your answer to Jesus?

- What was your sense of Jesus as he asked the question, and as you answered him?

- What was Jesus' reaction to your answer?

- If Jesus asked you what you want again right now, would you have a different answer? Why or why not?

- What does your answer to Jesus tell you about yourself? What you value? What you need?

[End]

WOMAN CAUGHT IN ADULTERY

Scripture Reference: John 8:1-11

Themes: Sin, Shame, Guilt, Forgiveness

SNEAK PEEK

Your students are invited to experience this meditation as the woman caught in adultery. They'll hear themselves shamed and accused and then loved and forgiven.

BELLS AND WHISTLES

- Imaginative Prayer Treasure Chest (refer to page 37)

- Pile of stones

RUNDOWN

1. Slow Down (refer to page 44)

2. Read Imaginative Prayer Meditation.

3. Offer students quiet space for reflection.

4. Optional Reflection/Journal Questions

IMAGINATIVE PRAYER MEDITATION

Your worst nightmare is coming true. Half naked, you're being hauled through the streets like a piece of trash by men who are angry and vengeful. As a woman, you feel vulnerable and defenseless. Also, you know they have a right to their accusations. You're guilty of a terrible crime.

You've committed adultery. You've betrayed your husband and marriage by having sex with another man. And you've been caught. Word apparently leaked out. Someone saw you and reported what they saw. Temple leaders barged into your home and actually caught you in bed with this other man. You were pulled out of bed and out through the streets with only a thin blanket to cover your nakedness. Your face is hot with shame and humiliation. You want to hide or die.

Suddenly, you realize you probably *will* die. The punishment for adultery is death by stoning. They'll make you stand in a public place and circle around you, yelling insults and throwing stones at your body until you die.

Hot tears run down your face. Your breath is ragged and you've never been so afraid. Now the journey is over. The small crowd of men abruptly stops and then circles around you. You feel small and helpless, dirty and lost.

Someone yells out, "Jesus, this woman was found in bed with a man she's not married to. The law says to stone her. What do you say?"

This man, Jesus, looks at you with gentle, sad eyes. Those eyes look very different from the other pairs of eyes glaring at you. Jesus bends down and starts drawing in the dirt. Even in the midst of your fear and shame, you want to touch his hand as he draws, but you don't move.

The men keep questioning Jesus over and over again. What does he think should be done with you? Eventually he stands up and says, "Go ahead and stone her. Whoever is perfect and hasn't sinned himself should throw the first stone." Then he bends down again and continues drawing.

Everything gets very quiet. The air itself seems to change. Slowly, the men with angry eyes and voices begin to leave. Eventually, you're left alone with Jesus.

Jesus stands up and those gentle eyes look at you once again. "Where are the men who accuse you?" he asks.

"They're gone," you weakly reply.

Jesus tenderly takes your tear-stained face in his hands and smiles. Then he says, "I don't accuse you, either. I love you, and I want you to live! Go, know yourself as beloved, and you'll be free to really live." **(Pause a moment.)**

You turn and wander away, slowly walking back to your home. Jesus' words have touched a broken part of you.

As you hug your blanket a little tighter, you recall his gentle face and hear his words again. "I don't accuse you, either. I love you, and I want you to live! Go, know yourself as beloved, and you'll be free to really live."

OPTIONAL REFLECTION/JOURNAL QUESTIONS

- Think of a time you were caught doing something wrong. What feelings did you experience?

- How do you think Jesus looks at you when you've sinned? How did he look at the woman in this meditation?

- Remember a time you were afraid. Where was Jesus? Did he seem nearby or far away?

- How do you think Jesus responds to your fear?

- How did it feel for you to have Jesus not accuse you, but tell you to go and live?

[End]

DEATH OF LAZARUS

Scripture Reference: John 11:1-35

Themes: Grief, Compassion

SNEAK PEEK

There are two different exercises in this book that deal with this particular passage. The other one is found in chapter 11. It's called *Resurrection of Lazarus* (see page 132), and it covers the miracle of Jesus raising Lazarus from the dead.

This exercise, *Death of Lazarus*, will cover the part of the passage leading up to the point when Jesus weeps. It focuses on Jesus' emotions and compassion. As you lead or when you talk about this exercise beforehand, don't mention the title or the name "Lazarus." It's helpful for the students NOT to know the whole story.

BELLS AND WHISTLES

- Imaginative Prayer Treasure Chest (refer to page 37)

RUNDOWN

1. Slow Down (refer to page 44)

2. Read Imaginative Prayer Meditation.

3. Offer students quiet space for reflection.

4. Optional Reflection/Journal Questions

IMAGINATIVE PRAYER MEDITATION

You are traveling with Jesus when a messenger arrives and says to Jesus, "Your friend is sick; please come." You watch Jesus' reaction. He seems untroubled by the news and appears to be in no hurry to visit his friend. This seems odd to you—especially when Jesus stays put for the next two days, teaching, resting, and praying.

One morning, as you're all having breakfast, Jesus announces that his friend is dead. He says it matter-of-factly. You're puzzled. This makes no sense. How can this be? Why didn't Jesus do something?

Now Jesus makes his way to the city where his friend lived. He is met by one of his friend's sisters, who says to him, "Jesus, if you had been here, my brother would not have died." A little while later, the other sister arrives and says the same thing, "Jesus, if you had been here, my brother would not have died." You notice the sister's eyes are red and puffy from crying. Now you hear the wails of friends and relatives as they mourn this man's death.

Why didn't Jesus get here sooner? Now will Jesus do something? But what can he do? His friend has been dead for four days. But surely Jesus is going to do *something*.

As you watch Jesus and hope for a miracle, you notice his face. His eyes look very, very sad. Then you hear a deep, troubled sigh followed by a painful moan. These sounds are coming from Jesus! You notice his shoulders as they shudder. You hear his sigh and moans become tears, and then the tears become great sobs. Jesus weeps. Deeply moved by the pain and anguish of these people, and troubled by the reality of death, Jesus weeps.

Jesus' love for his friend, his friend's sisters, and all who mourn the loss of this man is communicated through his tears. Jesus' love is demonstrated by his willingness to be with the people during their time of sorrow, confusion, and grief.

OPTIONAL REFLECTION/JOURNAL QUESTIONS

- What does this story tell you about Jesus?

- Does anything in this story surprise you about Jesus' tears?

- What do you think you'd be feeling as you saw Jesus weeping?

- What does this story tell you about feeling sadness and sorrow?

- How does knowing that Jesus feels and embraces your pain to the point of tears make you feel about Jesus?

- You're invited to go back to a place of pain in your imagination. Focus on Jesus' presence with you—imagine Jesus loving you and carrying your pain and sorrow, hurting with you and for you.

[End]

CHAPTER 11

GOSPEL TIME—MIRACLES
[EIGHT EXERCISES]

JESUS WALKS ON WATER

Scripture Reference: Matthew 14:22-27

Themes: Trust, Faith

SNEAK PEEK

This is one of two exercises in which Jesus walks on the water. In this exercise the student sees Jesus walking on the water, notices the disciples' fear, and hears Jesus' response, "Take courage! It is I. Don't be afraid." In the other exercise taken from this passage, *Peter Walks on Water* (page 117), students are asked to put themselves in Peter's place.

BELLS AND WHISTLES

- Imaginative Prayer Treasure Chest (refer to page 37)

- Visual of ocean/stormy seas

RUNDOWN

1. Slow Down (refer to page 44)

2. Read Imaginative Prayer Meditation.

3. Offer students quiet space for reflection.

4. Optional Reflection/Journal Questions

IMAGINATIVE PRAYER MEDITATION

You are in a boat with the disciples. Jesus sent all of you away so he could be alone. You've been in the boat for a couple of hours now. Everyone has taken turns rowing, but you haven't gone too far yet, maybe a mile or two. It's hard to tell exactly how far because a mist is rising from the surface of the water, making it impossible to see. All you know for sure is that the wind and the waves have been against you ever since you left the shore.

You are tired, very tired. When you're not rowing, you try to grab a little sleep. No one is in a good mood. You wish you were with Jesus back on the shore. You wonder why he sent you all ahead. What is Jesus doing right now?

It feels as though you're going nowhere; frustration and anger rise within you. It's your turn to row again. You move to your place and angrily snatch the oars. Soon you settle into a steady rowing pattern, and your mind begins to drift into a dreamlike trance.

You hear someone say, "Look, what is that?" You snap back to the present and look where the person is pointing. You strain to see what's causing the commotion, but it's hard to see anything in this fog. Then another disciple cries out, "Look, it's a ghost!" You wonder what's going on.

You stop rowing. Once again you look in the direction where the two disciples are pointing. You see what appears to be a human figure walking on the water—but that's impossible! Someone is out there—or something. Maybe they're standing in a boat. You don't believe it's a ghost.

As you strain to get a closer look, it's obvious that there is no other boat. Whatever that figure is, it's definitely standing on the surface of the water. Fear starts to stir within you, and you can see it on the faces of the others, too—fear, uncertainty, and confusion.

You hear a voice coming from the figure on the water, "Take courage! It is I. Don't be afraid." You repeat the words to yourself—"Take courage! It is I. Don't be afraid." You know that voice. It's Jesus! Jesus is speaking to you in this time of fear, confusion, and anxiety, "It is I. Don't be afraid."

Sit with these words. What do they mean to you? What feelings do they stir within you? Can you believe and embrace them deep within? Why or why not?

"Take courage! It is I. Don't be afraid." Ponder these words of Jesus as they are spoken to you in this moment, with all that is happening within you and in the current circumstances of your life.

OPTIONAL REFLECTION/JOURNAL QUESTIONS

- What does fear feel like for you?

- How do you respond to fear?

- What does Jesus' ability to walk on water tell you about Jesus?

- How does Jesus' ability to walk on water make you feel about Jesus? Why?

- If you were afraid and you heard Jesus say to you, "Take courage! It is I. Don't be afraid," what impact would that have on your life?

- The ability to take courage and not be afraid is based on one's view of Jesus. What do you know or what have you experienced in your life that would make it easy for you to trust Jesus or make it difficult to trust Jesus?

[End]

PETER WALKS ON WATER

Scripture Reference: Matthew 14:22-32

Themes: Trust, Failure

SNEAK PEEK

This is the second Jesus-walking-on-the-water exercise. In this one the students watch as Peter walks to Jesus on the water. Then the students are asked to put themselves into the role of Peter and walk on the water to Jesus.

BELLS AND WHISTLES

- Imaginative Prayer Treasure Chest (refer to page 37)

RUNDOWN

1. Slow Down (refer to page 44)

2. Read Imaginative Prayer Meditation.

3. Offer students quiet space for reflection.

4. Optional Reflection/Journal Questions

IMAGINATIVE PRAYER MEDITATION

You are in a boat with the disciples. Jesus sent all of you away so he could be alone. You've been in the boat for a couple of hours now. Everyone has taken turns rowing, but you haven't gone too far yet, maybe a mile or two. It's hard to tell exactly how far because there's a mist arising from the surface of the water, making it impossible to see. All you know for sure is that the wind and the waves have been against you ever since you left the shore.

You are tired, very tired. When you're not rowing, you try to grab a little sleep. No one is in a good mood. You wish you were with Jesus back on the shore. You wonder why he sent you all ahead. What is Jesus doing right now?

It feels as though you're going nowhere; frustration and anger rise within you. It's your turn to row again. You move to your place and angrily snatch the oars. Soon you settle into a steady rowing pattern, and your mind begins to drift into a dreamlike trance.

You hear someone say, "Look, what is that?" You snap back to the present and look where the person is pointing. You strain to see what's causing the commotion, but it's hard to see anything in this fog. Then another disciple cries out, "Look, it's a ghost!" You wonder what's going on.

You stop rowing. Once again you look in the direction where the two disciples are pointing. You see what appears to be a human figure walking on the water—but that's impossible! Someone is out there—or something. Maybe they're standing in a boat. You don't believe it's a ghost.

As you strain to get a closer look, it's obvious there's no other boat. Whatever that figure is, it's definitely standing on the surface of the water. Fear stirs within you, and you can see it on the faces of the others, too—fear, uncertainty, and confusion.

You hear a voice coming from the figure on the water, "Take courage! It is I. Don't be afraid." You repeat the words to yourself—"Take courage! It is I. Don't be afraid." You know that voice. It's Jesus! Jesus is speaking to you in this time of fear, confusion, and anxiety, "It is I. Don't be afraid." The words bring a mixture of comfort and confusion. Jesus is walking on the *water*.

You begin to think through all of this. As you do, you hear the irritating voice of Peter, "Lord, if it is you, tell me to come out to you on the water." *Peter, what is your problem?* you think to yourself. *Why do you have to be so dramatic about everything?*

As you're thinking these thoughts, you hear Jesus' response to Peter's request: "Come." You watch as Peter puts one leg over the side of the boat, then the other. You see him standing—and then he's *walking* on the water!

What are you feeling? What is going on in your mind as Peter is out on the water walking toward Jesus? What does Peter's ability to walk on water tell you about Jesus? How does that make you feel about Jesus? **(Allow significant pause.)**

You continue to watch as Peter moves farther and farther away from the boat and closer to Jesus. You see him take his eyes off Jesus and start looking to the right and left. You see him begin to sink. You hear Peter cry out, "Save me!" and you watch as Jesus reaches out and saves him.

Now put yourself in Peter's place. You see a figure on the water and believe it to be Jesus. Then you hear yourself saying, "Lord, if it is you, tell me to come out to you on the water."

You hear Jesus' response, "Come." All the disciples are watching you and wondering what you're going to do. You move to the side of the boat and swing first one leg over and then the other. You're balancing on the side of the boat while it rocks back and forth. You see Jesus out on the water in front of you, waiting for you. You lock your eyes on him and place both feet on top of the water, while still sitting on the edge of the boat.

Keeping your eyes fixed on Jesus, you try to stand…you're standing. You're standing on the water! You take one step, then another, and another—now you're walking on the water!

What are you feeling? What is going on in your heart and head? How does that make you feel about Jesus? How does it make you feel about you? **(Allow significant pause.)**

You continue to move farther and farther away from the boat and closer to Jesus. Then you feel the spray of water on your face and the wind blowing through your hair. For the first time, you take your eyes off Jesus and start looking to the right and left. You notice the wind and the waves and immediately begin to sink. You cry out, "Save me!" and Jesus reaches out and saves you.

Ponder the various parts of this experience—walking on the water, sinking, being saved by Jesus. What feelings were you experiencing? What can you learn about you and about Jesus?

OPTIONAL REFLECTION/JOURNAL QUESTIONS

- In terms of your feelings, what was the difference between watching Peter walk on the water and you walking on the water?

- How did you feel about Jesus during your time out on the water?

- What were you feeling as you sank?

- How do you think Jesus felt about you when you sank? Why?

- What did you learn about Jesus when you sank?

- How did you feel after Jesus rescued you?

- What can your sinking experience teach you about how to deal with failure in your life—those times when we're sinking below the surface and aren't going to make it or when we're overwhelmed by the circumstances of our lives?

- What makes it difficult for you to keep your eyes on Jesus?

- What did you learn about yourself and about Jesus as you were walking on the water?

- What did you learn about yourself and about Jesus when you sank and Jesus rescued you?

[End]

JESUS CALMS THE STORM

Scripture Reference: Mark 4:35-41

Theme: Fear

SNEAK PEEK

This exercise puts students in the boat with the disciples and Jesus. A storm grows fierce and fear begins to consume everyone in the boat except Jesus, who is fast asleep. This passage gives the students the opportunity to look at fear and at times in their lives when they may have felt as though Jesus wasn't there for them.

There are two exercises based on this passage. They can be used separately or together. This one stops when the person in the boat has been overcome by fear. The other exercise, *Resting with Jesus* (on page 122), invites students to rest with Jesus while the storm rages.

BELLS AND WHISTLES

- Imaginative Prayer Treasure Chest (refer to page 37)

- A sound track of a stormy ocean

- An ocean drum

RUNDOWN

1. Slow Down (refer to page 44)

2. Read Imaginative Prayer Meditation.

3. Offer students quiet space for reflection.

4. Optional Reflection/Journal Questions

IMAGINATIVE PRAYER MEDITATION

You are with the disciples standing near the Sea of Galilee. You can hear the lapping of the water. Feel the moisture in the air and the blowing of a gentle breeze. You hear Jesus call out, "Let's cross to the other side of the lake." Jesus is already in the boat, so you and the other disciples quickly get in. Some of the disciples begin to row, and the boat slowly moves away from the shore.

Jesus takes a place in the back of the boat, grabs a cushion for his head, and lies down. As you and the disciples continue across the lake, you begin to feel the force of the wind picking up. You notice the waves are beginning to build in height and intensity. As the waves continue to grow, they start crashing into the boat, causing huge amounts of water to fill the boat.

You look at the faces of the disciples: Simon, Andrew, James, and John, fishermen who grew up on the lake. You see fear in their eyes and hear panic in their voices. "Start getting some of this water out of the boat!" they shout. Your mind is racing, fear is rising and gaining control over you as each wave crashes into the boat, bringing with it more water.

You suddenly remember Jesus—man of God, powerful, caring, concerned, and involved. You turn to see him, seeking to draw strength, courage, and hope from him. But he's asleep. Jesus is sleeping while you and the disciples are facing certain death. Anger begins to rise within you. Doesn't Jesus care? Your fear begins to birth panic and you rush over to Jesus, frantically shaking him and shouting, "Don't you care that we're about to drown?"

Jesus awakens. "Quiet down," he says. The wind and waves stop. He then looks at you and the rest of the disciples saying, "Why are you so afraid? Do you still have no faith in me?"

OPTIONAL REFLECTION/JOURNAL QUESTIONS

- Spend some time with this experience. Think through this event and Jesus' words to you: "Why are you so afraid? Do you still have no faith in me?" Have you ever been in a difficult situation that was out of your control and felt as though Jesus wasn't there or he didn't care? How did that feel?

- How did that make you think or feel about God?

- Bring your thoughts and feelings to Jesus.

- What are your greatest fears?

- What is it about these things that make you afraid?

- How does it feel to remember those things that make you afraid?

- What do you think Jesus feels about these things and about your fear?

- What does this story tell you about Jesus' power?

- How does seeing Jesus' power displayed make you feel?

- Have you ever seen or experienced the power of Jesus in your life?

- No matter how you answered that last question, how do you feel about your response?

- Spend some time talking to Jesus about all of this.

[End]

RESTING WITH JESUS

Scripture Reference: Mark 4:35-41

Themes: Rest, Trust, Peace

SNEAK PEEK

There are two exercises based on this passage. The other one is called *Jesus Calms the Storm*, found on page 120. If you'll be using the two together, then this one should be part two. You can break up the exercises by giving time for the students to reflect on the first before moving on to the second.

This exercise begins exactly the same as part one, but then takes an abrupt change of direction. Once again it puts the students in the boat with the disciples and Jesus. But as the storm grows fiercer, fear consumes everyone in the boat except for Jesus and your students. They choose not to give in to their fear, but rather draw close and trust in Jesus. This passage gives the students the opportunity to look at fear and what it means to trust. It also provides them with an opportunity to look back at their lives and see how they have (or haven't) been able to trust and rest in Jesus.

BELLS AND WHISTLES

- Imaginative Prayer Treasure Chest (refer to page 37)
- Pillow and/or blanket for each student
- Sound track of a stormy ocean
- Ocean drum

RUNDOWN

1. If you're using this as part two, explain to your students that they're about to revisit the story of Jesus in the boat, but this time they'll respond to the circumstances in a different way. If you're using this as a stand-alone exercise, no special instruction is needed.

2. Distribute the blankets and/or pillows and have the students get comfortable.

3. Slow Down (refer to page 44)

4. Read Imaginative Prayer Meditation.

5. Offer students quiet space for reflection.

6. Optional Reflection/Journal Questions

IMAGINATIVE PRAYER MEDITATION

You are with the disciples standing near the Sea of Galilee. You can hear the lapping of the water. Feel the moisture in the air and the blowing of a gentle breeze. You hear Jesus call out, "Let's cross to the other side of the lake." Jesus is already in the boat, so you and the other disciples quickly get in. Some of the disciples begin to row, and the boat slowly moves away from the shore.

Jesus takes a place in the back of the boat, grabs a cushion for his head, and lies down. As you and the disciples continue across the lake, you begin to feel the force of the wind picking up. You notice the waves are beginning to build in height and intensity. As the waves continue to grow, they start crashing into the boat, causing huge amounts of water to fill the boat.

You look at the faces of the disciples: Simon, Andrew, James, and John, fishermen who grew up on the lake. You see fear in their eyes and hear panic in their voices. "Start getting some of this water out of the boat!" they shout. Your mind is racing, fear is rising and gaining more and more control over you as each wave crashes into the boat, bringing with it more water.

You suddenly remember Jesus—man of God, powerful, caring, concerned, and involved. You turn to see him, seeking to draw strength, courage, and hope from him. But he's asleep. Jesus is sleeping while you and the disciples are facing certain death. Anger begins to rise within you. Doesn't Jesus care? Your fear begins to birth panic.

However, instead of allowing anger, fear, and panic to have their way with you, you decide to lie down next to Jesus. Carefully crawling on your hands and knees, you slowly move to where Jesus is sleeping. Wave after wave crashes over the boat and sprays you with water, but you continue to crawl closer and closer to Jesus, fixing your eyes on his peaceful face and relaxed body. As you get close to Jesus, you see him open an eye and pat the place next to him. You move into that place and lie down.

The storm rages on and the waves crash, tossing the boat high in the air one minute and submerging it beneath the water the next. The boat is taking on more and more water, the spray of the waves lands on you, demanding that you be consumed by your situation. But instead of panic, you notice a peace rising up within as you settle down next to Jesus. You feel the weight of his arm as he drapes it over you and draws you near. You lie next to Jesus, while the others are rushing around frantically, overcome by fear and panic. The circumstances remain the same, but you're with Jesus, and Jesus is with you.

Spend the next few minutes lying close to Jesus—maybe even falling asleep next to him—as the wind and waves continue to roar.

OPTIONAL REFLECTION/JOURNAL QUESTIONS

These first three questions are for those who did both exercises:

- How was this experience different from the first exercise?

- What made the difference?

- What changed in the story?

- How did being with Jesus change how you felt about the storm?

- What are some stormy areas in your life right now?

- Spend some time talking with Jesus about these storms and how you can learn to rest in him or be bold enough to wake him.

- Have you ever experienced the peace that comes from being able to rest with Jesus?

- No matter how you answered that last question, how do you feel about your response?

- What helped or what hindered you from resting with Jesus?

[End]

SHE TOUCHES HIS ROBE

Scripture Reference: Mark 5:25-34

Themes: Healing, Faith, Courage

SNEAK PEEK

As the listeners enter the story of a woman who has suffered from severe bleeding for 12 years, this exercise will invite your students to reach out and touch the robe of Jesus and experience their own healing.

BELLS AND WHISTLES

- Imaginative Prayer Treasure Chest (refer to page 37)

- Ambient music

- Fabric to represent Jesus' robes. Lay it on an altar or drape it over a cross.

RUNDOWN

1. Slow Down (refer to page 44)

2. Read Imaginative Prayer Meditation.

3. Offer students quiet space for reflection.

4. Optional Reflection/Journal Questions

IMAGINATIVE PRAYER MEDITATION

You've been sick for 12 long years. You have a hemorrhaging condition, which means your body is always bleeding. The doctors can't seem to make it stop. You used to believe the doctors would eventually help you get better. Sure, they've tried all kinds of things to stop the bleeding, but nothing has helped. And sometimes their treatments make the bleeding worse or cause cramping or make you throw up. But the doctors kept trying new and horrible "cures" until you finally ran out of money. Now no one tries anything.

You live alone in a little shack, and you have no real friends. Everyone knows about your bleeding condition, and they consider you unclean. No one dares to touch you. They act as though they're afraid they'll catch whatever you have.

Homes and families surround you, yet you don't belong to any of the lives you see. You're an observer, not a participant. There's an ache deep inside of you that has nothing to do with the bleeding, but everything to do with being left out and left alone.

Once in a while, someone touches that lonely spot in you. It happened about a week ago. You were listening to a man named Jesus as he spoke to a crowd of people. He's called the Healer. Jesus' words and voice touched that aching spot in you, and you haven't been able to stop thinking about him. Since then you've had the same wonderful dream three different times, where Jesus comes to you and takes your hand. But when you tell him you're unclean, he simply smiles. Then you wake up crying. You're starting to believe in healing again, but you're so afraid to hope.

Today, you're walking along the road when a crowd of people approaches. This great mass of people is trying to make its way along a road that's much too small to accommodate its size. Then you realize the people are surrounding Jesus. The Healer is here! Your heart leaps as you see him pass by. *If only I can touch his garment, I'll be healed.* You work your way into the crowd and toward him. Suddenly, he's walking just ahead of you. You reach out and—holding your breath—you touch the edge of his robe as a single word escapes your lips: "Please."

In that moment everything changes. You stop walking, and your mouth drops open when you realize the bleeding has stopped. There's strength in your body that wasn't there before. There's energy rather than fatigue. You've been healed.

But Jesus stops walking, too. He turns and asks who touched him. Now you're afraid. You try to remain silent, and you don't dare lift your eyes from the dusty ground beneath your feet. But Jesus keeps looking around. You know he'll find you. So finally you move forward, fall to your knees, and tearfully tell Jesus your story. You tell him about your long illness, and you tell him why you touched his robe. Jesus crouches down and lifts your chin until you're face-to-face with him. He smiles and takes your hand. It's just like your dream! You begin to cry as somehow the world disappears and the look and touch of Jesus heal you in a second way. That lonely ache finally disappears.

OPTIONAL REFLECTION/JOURNAL QUESTIONS

- What feelings came up for you during this meditation?

- Would it be difficult for you to do what this woman did? Why or why not?

- This woman was healed emotionally and physically. What healing do you desire? Share your need with Jesus.

- Which need touched you more deeply—the physical or the emotional need? Why?

[End]

THE BLIND BEGGAR

Scripture Reference: Mark 10:46-52

Themes: Desire, Faith

SNEAK PEEK

This exercise is inspired by the interchange between a blind beggar and Jesus. Your students are invited to place themselves in the role of the beggar and answer Jesus' question, "What do you want me to do for you?"

BELLS AND WHISTLES

- Imaginative Prayer Treasure Chest (refer to page 37)

- A visual of a homeless person

RUNDOWN

1. Slow Down (refer to page 44)

2. Read Imaginative Prayer Meditation.

3. Offer students quiet space for reflection.

4. Optional Reflection/Journal Questions

IMAGINATIVE PRAYER MEDITATION

You're a blind beggar sitting by the side of the road. You sit there alone, quietly holding out a cup that silently asks for money—asks for help. Sitting in the same spot every day, you survive heat, rain, and dust. But even worse than enduring these weather conditions, sometimes you feel invisible. People constantly walk by your spot, but they usually don't notice there's a human being in the midst of the rags you wear.

Only occasionally do you hear the clink of a coin as it's dropped into the cup. Once in a great while, someone may offer a kind word or a touch, but this is very rare. More often, you're mistreated, teased, or abused. Sometimes the money you've collected is even stolen or scattered on the street, forcing you to scramble on your hands and knees to find what you so desperately need.

You have an old, thin blanket to wrap up in. It's full of holes, so the cold air easily reaches your bare skin and keeps your muscles clenched and tight. Today the air is quite cold and there's a strong breeze; but the sun is also shining, and it's really quite beautiful outside. However, you can't see the beauty, and the sun isn't offering much warmth.

It's been very slow and quiet on the road today. Not much foot traffic at all. When people do walk by, they do so quickly because of the cold. There are no coins in your cup.

From off in the distance, you begin to hear voices. It sounds as though lots of people are coming this way. *Please, let there be help for me in this crowd. May someone give me what I need today,* you pray. You hear the name Jesus, and your heart starts thumping loudly. Jesus' name is well known, even to people who have to sit on the side of the road all day. He is the Healer. From somewhere deep inside your desperate soul, a cry goes up: "Jesus, help me! Please, Jesus, help me!" You yell and yell and seem unable to stop.

A coin is dropped in the cup as someone hisses at you to shut up and stop yelling at Jesus. "No!" you cry, throwing the cup down. "No! Not money—Jesus! I need Jesus!" Again people tell you to quiet down and stop making a scene. Don't

bother the Teacher. Stop being a nuisance. Sit quietly. Beg silently. But you won't be silenced.

Suddenly, someone grabs your arm and says, "Cheer Up! On your feet! He's calling you." You jump up excitedly, throw your blanket on the ground, and half-run, half-walk into the middle of the crowd. People make a path for you. The same ones who shushed you now guide you toward Jesus.

Jesus reaches out and grabs your worn and weathered hands. He gently holds them and asks with great compassion in his voice, "What do you want me to do for you?" The crowd becomes silent as you consider your answer.

What *do* you want from Jesus? Look inside yourself. What do you want? What do you need? Take your time before answering Jesus' question. **(Allow significant pause.)** As you answer the question, notice Jesus. His touch, his voice, his presence with you. How does Jesus respond to your request?

OPTIONAL REFLECTION/JOURNAL QUESTIONS

- What were some of your feelings during the exercise? Feelings about you, about the crowd, about Jesus?

- Did your feelings change during the exercise? If so, how?

- Did anything surprise you? If so, how did that affect you?

- Was it easy or difficult for you to find your answer for Jesus? To find words to express your answer? To actually say those words? Why?

- How did Jesus respond to your request? What do you notice about him as he listens, as he responds?

[End]

HEALING THE LEPER

Scripture Reference: Luke 5:12-13

Themes: Compassion, Acceptance

SNEAK PEEK

In this exercise the students will have the opportunity to just sit and rest in the reality of God's love for them just as they are.

BELLS AND WHISTLES

- Imaginative Prayer Treasure Chest (refer to page 37)
- Candles
- Images of people considered the "lepers" of our culture
- Paper and writing tools for debriefing

RUNDOWN

1. Slow Down (refer to page 44)
2. Read Imaginative Prayer Meditation.
3. Offer students quiet space for reflection.
4. Optional Reflection/Journal Questions

IMAGINATIVE PRAYER MEDITATION

You're walking with Jesus—or rather following him—down a pathway in the city. It's the afternoon, and the sun hangs high in the sky. You feel its warmth upon your face, and it feels good. There's even a slight breeze blowing. It's a warm, beautiful day.

You hear a voice up ahead crying out, "Unclean, unclean!" You already know what's coming—the smell of rotting flesh and the image of disfigured hands, feet, and face come to your mind, along with open, infected sores and oozing pus. The voice belongs to a leper. Those with leprosy must announce their presence to passersby because if someone comes within close proximity of a leper, it makes the clean person unclean and unable to be involved in the religious services for a period of time. Because of this rule, people routinely shun lepers; their lives are often devoid of human contact. They're even forced to live outside the city.

As the voice of the leper grows louder and louder, you prepare yourself for the sights and smells you're about to experience—you know they'll haunt you the rest of today and possibly part of the night. Jesus is ahead of you a little ways, and he stops walking when he reaches the leper. You watch in disbelief as the leper approaches Jesus and falls on his knees at Jesus' feet. This is wrong! Lepers are supposed to keep their distance. You hear the leper's voice, desperate and pleading, "Lord, if you are willing, you can make me clean." You think to yourself, *That's true; Jesus can heal this person.* In fact, when have you ever seen Jesus *not* heal someone who's asked him to do so?

You stand there waiting and watching for the miracle. But Jesus doesn't heal the leper right away. You see something even more astonishing. Jesus, the Son of God, the Holy One of Israel, reaches out his hand and *touches* this leper. He touches this disfigured, contagious , pus-oozing individual. And Jesus does this *before*—not after—he heals the man. Jesus, filled with care and concern, touches this untouchable person lovingly, tenderly, and gently.

Then, without removing his hand from the leper, Jesus says, "I am willing; be clean!" You are awestruck, dumbfounded by what has taken place. Tears well up in your eyes, but not because of the miracle you expected to happen. What has touched you so deeply is Jesus' willingness to touch the leper with such loving care and tenderness. You wonder, you hope, you struggle to believe—*If Jesus is willing to touch the leper, maybe he's willing to touch me, too. Maybe Jesus is willing to embrace me just as I am, with my struggles, with my wounds, with my junk. Maybe Jesus would touch me, would love me just as I am.*

As you're wondering about all of this, Jesus makes his way over to you. He stands before you and says, "I am willing," then wraps his arms around you. "I am willing. I love you."

Just sit for the next few moments and focus on Jesus' love for you.

OPTIONAL REFLECTION/JOURNAL QUESTIONS

- How does it make you feel to know that Jesus can and does love you just as you are—right here, right now. Write a letter expressing this to Jesus.

- How does this amazing love of God make you feel about yourself?

- What was it like to just sit and focus on the fact that God loves you?

- Is it easy or difficult to believe Jesus loves you like that? Why?

- As you watch Jesus touch the one with leprosy, who in our world is the unclean, the rejected, the outsider?

- How did you feel as you watched Jesus love the one with leprosy? How are you drawn to respond to the "unclean" in our world?

[End]

RESURRECTION OF LAZARUS

Scripture Reference: John 11:1-44

Theme: Power

SNEAK PEEK

There are two different exercises that deal with this passage—the other one is found in chapter 10. It's called *Death of Lazarus* (see page 113). This exercise focuses on the end of the story (the resurrection of Lazarus), while the other one covers up to the time when Jesus weeps. You may do both exercises back-to-back, or just do one of them.

As you lead or when you talk about this exercise beforehand, don't mention the title or the name "Lazarus." It's helpful for the students NOT to know the whole story.

BELLS AND WHISTLES

- Imaginative Prayer Treasure Chest (refer to page 37)

RUNDOWN

1. Slow Down (refer to page 44)

2. Read Imaginative Prayer Meditation.

3. Offer students quiet space for reflection.

4. Optional Reflection/Journal Questions

IMAGINATIVE PRAYER MEDITATION

You stand near the tomb where the dead body of Jesus' friend has been placed. He's been dead for four days. The scene is disturbing. People are wailing un-controllably. Both of the dead man's sisters have come to Jesus, saying, "If you had been here, my brother would not have died." You believe this as well, yet you also know that Jesus didn't come right after he heard the news of his friend's illness. You know he waited two whole days before coming.

You're confused, confused by Jesus' delay, yet further and more deeply confused by the words Jesus has spoken since the day he found out his friend was sick:

This sickness is not unto death.

It is for the glory of God.

At first these words seemed encouraging, hopeful, like something great was going to take place. Jesus' friend was not going to die! But yesterday, while on your way to the house of Jesus' friend, he said, "My friend is dead."

Wait a second, you thought to yourself, *didn't Jesus just say that his friend was not going to die?* But you said nothing. Then Jesus made a statement that was even more shocking than the last, "I'm glad I wasn't there."

Did he really say that? He's glad he wasn't there to help? To heal his friend the way he's healed countless others? This isn't right. What's going on here? This is crazy talk!

You still believe Jesus is going to do something, but your hope quickly fades as you watch him weep for his friend. Jesus is weeping. Jesus' love for his friend is evident, but you start to think that some things are even beyond Jesus' power. So why did Jesus delay? Why did he say this was a good thing and for God's glory? This doesn't make sense.

You now watch as Jesus dries his eyes and, though still visibly shaken, begins to take control of the situation. He orders the stone to be removed from the entrance to the tomb. Several object, but Jesus ignores them. Soon, the stone is moved away. Jesus turns to speak to those who are gathered, friends and family, "Did I not tell you that if you believed, you would see the glory of God?"

What is Jesus up to? His friend has been dead for *four* days. But you continue watching as Jesus prays. Then he calls out in a loud voice, "Come out!" And his friend comes forward—alive and well.

OPTIONAL REFLECTION/JOURNAL QUESTIONS

- What were you feeling as you became a part of this story?

- Which of Jesus' words surprised you? Shocked you?

- How did your feelings toward Jesus change as the story progressed?

- What does the story tell us about Jesus' power?

- How might knowing and believing in the power of Jesus impact your life?

- If Jesus is so powerful, then why do bad things still happen? Why do people still die?

- Does knowing about the power of Jesus help you to trust and depend on him? Why or why not?

- How could your belief in Jesus' power impact how you pray and what you pray about?

[End]

CHAPTER 12

GOSPEL TIME—HOLY WEEK
[THREE EXERCISES]

FOOT WASHING

Scripture Reference: John 13:1-5

Theme: Significance

SNEAK PEEK

This exercise involves foot washing. The students will have their feet washed and imagine that Jesus is doing the washing. At the end of the foot washing, the person washing each student's feet will whisper something into the student's ear that expresses the uniqueness of who they are. (Note: Having same-sex foot-washing pairs (males washing males' feet, females washing females' feet) is probably a good thing—a *really* good thing.)

BELLS AND WHISTLES

* Imaginative Prayer Treasure Chest (refer to page 37)

* Towels, basins, containers for water (use warm water, if at all possible). Have everything ready before the students arrive. However, you may want to keep the items hidden if you don't want to tip your hand as to what's about to happen.

* Soft music without lyrics would be nice. It helps to fill the silence for those who are waiting, and it also makes it more difficult for them to overhear what's being whispered to the other students.

RUNDOWN

1. If possible, let your foot washers know ahead of time whose feet they'll be washing. Give them the following instructions:

   * Wash others' feet as if you were Jesus. Don't rush. Be gentle. Treat each student as if she were the only one.

   * After washing a student's feet, walk over and whisper in his ear. What you say should be in harmony with the grace, tenderness,

and love of Jesus. The student will be imagining that you are Jesus speaking. Speak clearly and slowly. No preaching.

2. Remind your foot washers that they are to do this as Jesus would do. They should go slowly, gently. There's no need to rush. And when they speak to the students, they need to speak slowly and clearly. Treat each student as if she were the only one.

3. Read Imaginative Prayer Meditation.

4. Offer students quiet space for reflection.

5. Optional Reflection/Journal Questions

IMAGINATIVE PRAYER MEDITATION

(First, read aloud John 13:1-5 to your students.) Like the disciples, you'll be having your feet washed. Don't take off your shoes or socks just yet; someone will do this for you.

Before you get your feet washed, I want you to imagine that Jesus is taking off your shoes and socks and washing and drying your feet. And then keep imagining that it's Jesus who gets up, walks behind you, and whispers something into your ear.

Let's prepare ourselves to enter into this time. **(Go through the Slow Down, page 44, and then begin the foot washing.)**

OPTIONAL REFLECTION/JOURNAL QUESTIONS

• What was this experience like for you?

• How did it make you feel?

• What was going on in your mind as your feet were being washed, as someone whispered in your ear?

• Do you think it would be easier to wash someone else's feet or to have yours washed? Why?

[End]

GARDEN OF GETHSEMANE

Scripture References: Matthew 26:36-44; Hebrews 4:14-16

Theme: Honesty with God

SNEAK PEEK

This exercise looks at the honesty of Jesus as he prays in the Garden of Gethsemane. It also provides an opportunity for the students to look at the role of emotions and honesty in prayer.

BELLS AND WHISTLES

- Imaginative Prayer Treasure Chest (refer to page 37)

- A nighttime visual of the Garden of Gethsemane or a similar location, or a visual of Jesus praying in the garden

- A darkened room

RUNDOWN

1. Slow Down (refer to page 44)

2. Read Imaginative Prayer Meditation.

3. Offer students quiet space for reflection.

4. Optional Reflection/Journal Questions

IMAGINATIVE PRAYER MEDITATION

You are sitting in a room with Jesus and the disciples. You've just finished a special meal together. Earlier in the evening, Jesus washed your feet and the feet of all the disciples. Your mind is still processing the unusual events of this night when Jesus stands up, looks in your direction, and asks, "Will you come with me?" You stand and follow Jesus, silently wondering what's going on now.

It's dark and cold outside, and you're very tired. But how could you refuse Jesus' request? He has chosen you, performed miracles, taught you truth, and given a sense of purpose to your life. And even more than all of that, Jesus has loved you with an everlasting, nothing-can-separate-you kind of love. Jesus has given you a sense of value and significance that can never be taken away because it's based on who you are, not what you do. So although you're tired and worn out, you walk out into the night with Jesus, even though you really want to go to bed.

As you begin walking, Jesus turns to you and says, "I want you to be with me as I pray." You sense he doesn't want to be alone tonight. On countless other occasions he's gone off by himself to pray. But tonight he's asked you to accompany him; tonight he wants you there with him. You feel honored by his special request.

You walk together in silence. There is no one else around. It's very, very quiet. The only noise you hear is the sound of your footsteps in the leaves and Jesus' deep sighs. He seems troubled, anxious, even worried. You've never seen him act like this before. **(Pause a moment.)**

When you reach an olive orchard at the foot of a hill, Jesus stops and says to you, "Sit here and pray for me while I go over there and pray." Wow, Jesus wants *you* to pray for *him*. You sit down and lean back against a tree. The ground is cold, and your body feels achy and tired. Your eyelids seem to weigh a hundred pounds as you fight to stay awake and pray for Jesus.

As Jesus walks a little way away from you, it seems the weight of the world is pressing more and more upon him with each step. He walks very slowly. His shoulders are hunched. Then you see Jesus fall with his face to the ground. You hear his anguished sighs. You hear his voice as he begins to pray. His voice sounds troubled, almost desperate.

You hear him as he pleads with God, "My Father, if it is possible, may this cup be taken from me." Jesus is asking for God the Father's help. It sounds as though he's trying to get out of doing something. You don't know what Jesus is referring to, but you do know it must be something terrible, so stress-inducing that Jesus is now sweating drops of blood. **(Pause a moment.)**

You've heard Jesus pray before, but you've never heard him say anything like this. You also know Jesus always receives whatever he requests from the Lord. So you're convinced he will be freed from whatever he's struggling with right now. But then you hear Jesus conclude his prayer, "Yet not as I will, but as you will." Jesus is asking for something, but he's also saying to God, "You do what you think is best."

You watch and listen to Jesus as he prays this prayer three times, concluding each time with, "Yet not as I will, but as you will." You sit quietly, watching as Jesus struggles to trust God. You listen as Jesus honestly expresses his struggle to God in his prayer. You begin to wonder if it might be okay for you to be this honest with God about the things you struggle with, even those things that you believe God wants you to do. If Jesus can be honest with God, then maybe you can be honest with God, too.

OPTIONAL REFLECTION/JOURNAL QUESTIONS

- What does this story teach you about Jesus?

- How does this story affect your feelings regarding Jesus?

- How does this story affect your view of prayer and what can be said to God in prayer?

- What emotions does Jesus experience as he gets ready to go to the cross?

- What can Jesus' display of emotions tell us about our own emotions?

- Does Jesus still trust God, even though he's stressed and worried about going to the cross? Do you trust God with your concerns? Why or why not? Talk honestly to God about that.

- What does Jesus' example of honesty in prayer teach us about being honest in our prayers?

- Are there some things you need to be honest with God about—maybe something you know you need to do, but it's difficult, even frightening? Take some time and honestly express your feelings to Jesus. God listens, understands, and cares.

[End]

THE CRUCIFIXION

Scripture Reference: Matthew 27:11-66; John 19:1-42

Theme: Grief

SNEAK PEEK

This exercise is designed to help your students enter the familiar crucifixion story through the eyes of the spectators.

BELLS AND WHISTLES

- Imaginative Prayer Treasure Chest (refer to page 37)

- A cross or crucifix

- A crown of thorns

- Nails

- A mallet

- A spear

- A whip

RUNDOWN

1. Slow Down (refer to page 47)

2. Read Imaginative Prayer Meditation after instructing your students to begin as an observer. As the meditation progresses, you'll be instructing them to imaginatively become particular characters in the story and view a portion of the scene from their perspectives.

3. Give your students some quiet space for reflection, especially as indicated within the meditation.

4. Optional Reflection/Journal Questions

5. Following this exercise, you may want to consider leading your students in a time of communion.

IMAGINATIVE PRAYER MEDITATION

Jesus has been sentenced to death. Most of his closest friends have run away in fear and confusion. Jesus' body has been brutally beaten, bloodied, and bruised. He has been spit on and cursed at. A crown of thorns has been shoved onto his head, causing blood to stream down his face.

Now soldiers pull Jesus to his feet and force him to carry his cross to the place where they'll crucify him. He's exhausted. His body screams with pain. His muscles cramp and ache under the weight of the cross. He's silent as he walks. His breathing is labored. Watch as Jesus journeys to his death. **(Pause a moment.)**

At last they arrive at Skull Hill. Jesus' clothes are removed, spikes are pounded into his hands and feet, and the cross is dropped into place. He's in excruciating pain, and his humiliation is public. The soldiers laugh at him. People passing on the road make fun of Jesus, yelling at him and spitting on him some more. See Jesus' face. See the faces of those yelling at him, spitting on him. **(Pause a moment.)**

Some of the witnesses are grieving. Mary Magdalene is there. Put yourself in her place. **(Pause a moment.)**

You would follow Jesus into death itself, and so here you are standing as close to him as you can get. Jesus gave you a reason to live. He gave your life purpose and meaning. Without him, you'd be lost. You will be lost. You cry desperate tears as you watch the One you love suffer and die. You stand near Jesus for as long as possible. They'll have to drag you away. Remember his healing touch, his playful smile, and his voice full of strength and gentleness. Remember when you sat at his feet and listened to his life-giving words. Oh how you want to sit at his feet again. Instead, you stand at the foot of his cross. **(Pause a moment.)**

Jesus' mother is there, too. Put yourself in her place. **(Pause a moment.)**

Where else would you be? What are you feeling as you watch your oldest child die in this horrible, public way? This is the baby you gave birth to and cherished, the little boy you laughed and cried with, the One who owns your heart. When the angel told you not to be afraid, did the angel know this day would come? Did the angel know your heart would be broken like this? How does a mother watch her son die? **(Pause a moment.)**

And there is John, Jesus' best friend. Put yourself in his place. **(Pause a moment.)**

You've lived with Jesus for three years, eaten with him, traveled everywhere with him, laughed and cried with him. You've watched Jesus heal people and confront people. Jesus has loved, challenged, and confused you. He taught you what it means to really live, to experience adventure and true friendship. All you want is to continue your journey together. But it seems the journey is now coming to an end. You stand at the foot of his cross, confused, sad, and helpless. **(Pause a moment.)**

Which character do you most resonate with? Mary Magdalene, Jesus' mother, or John? Take a moment to enter the scene at the foot of the cross as One of these characters. Stand at the foot of Jesus' cross and look at the body of the One you love. **(Pause a moment.)**

Now the whole earth becomes dark. Jesus groans and cries out, "My God, my God, why have you forsaken me?" His cry is full of pain and anguish and it breaks your heart. You want to bring him down and take him away. You want to nurse his wounds and hold his head in your lap. The ache in your heart is so strong, you can barely breathe. Watching Jesus suffer is the worst thing you've ever experienced.

Jesus speaks one last time. "It is finished," he says. He bows his head and stops breathing. Suddenly there's an earthquake and a violent storm. Everyone else has left, but you can't go. You can't bring yourself to leave him there. Standing in the rain, you put your lips up to the bloody feet of Jesus and kiss him one last time. Then you slump to the ground. You have no sense of what to do now.

OPTIONAL REFLECTION/JOURNAL QUESTIONS

- What feelings did this meditation bring up for you?

- You're invited to stand at the foot of the cross and tell Jesus your thoughts and feelings. Allow him to look into your eyes as you share your heart.

- Give Jesus time to respond to you. What does he want to say? What do you see in his eyes?

- How do you respond when you feel overwhelmed, confused, or sad? How do you act? How do you feel?

- When you feel overwhelmed, confused, or sad, does God seem nearby or far away? Can you share with God why you feel that way? Allow God to respond to you.

[End]

N.T. TIME [TWO EXERCISES]

PETER AND CORNELIUS

Scripture Reference: Acts 10:1-48

Theme: Loving Others

SNEAK PEEK

This exercise is inspired by Peter's conversion, or complete change of perspective, to a further understanding of the gospel and its intended recipients. It's completely modern day, so if you want to tie it into the biblical story, read Acts 10 to your students following the exercise. Perhaps this exercise will encourage your students to look outside their comfort zones for places where God may be inviting them to display grace and acceptance.

BELLS AND WHISTLES

- Imaginative Prayer Treasure Chest (refer to page 37)

- Meet outside so it feels more park like or set up props to help the meeting room resemble a park.

- Image of a park bench

RUNDOWN

1. Slow Down (refer to page 44)

2. Read Imaginative Prayer Meditation.

3. Offer students quiet space for reflection.

4. Optional Reflection/Journal Questions

IMAGINATIVE PRAYER MEDITATION

You try to be a good Christian and love and obey God. You go to church all the time and are careful to keep yourself surrounded by good Christian friends. You believe doing so will help you make good choices and stay away from temptations. Sometimes it seems to help. Sometimes it doesn't. But you're trying. You're really trying.

Today you're sitting on a park bench alone. You're journaling and praying, when God suddenly shows up. This doesn't usually happen to you. In fact, it's never happened before. Typically, it would sound bizarre, yet pretty cool. However, God is telling you some hard news and you're having a tough time accepting it. God is telling you that the way you live your life isn't what God wants for you, and the way you look at the world isn't the way God looks at it. God wants to show you a different way to look at the world.

God talks to you about people who look different from you, who live differently than you do, and who even believe different things. God tells you these people are precious, loved, and highly valued. God asks you to stop living in your safe Christian circle. Stop offering your friendship only to people who look and act like you do.

Your brain can't take it in. You thought you were doing what God wanted! You're so confused. But God keeps talking, "Every time you show love to another person, every time you offer friendship to an outsider, you do that to me. To love me, you love others—that includes people who are different from you. Stop judging them. Just love them. Open your heart and you'll find it's not so hard most of the time. Although once in a while it can be really tough." God chuckles. "But I'll help you. Let others into your heart and life. You can learn from each other. They know me in ways you don't, and you know me in ways they don't. I created all of you and I love all of you. Love as I love."

God looks at you with compassion. Look into God's face and see the love there. "I want you to experience joy and freedom," God softly says. "Loving others freely is part of that. I speak to you out of a desire for you to experience a fuller life. May I sit with you on your bench? I'd love to hear your thoughts and feelings about all of this."

Do you want to talk? If so, invite God to share your bench and tell God what you're thinking and feeling. If not, be honest about that, too.

OPTIONAL REFLECTION/JOURNAL QUESTIONS

- Why do people tend to become friends with people who look and act like they do?

- Is it difficult for you to make friends with people who seem different from you? If so, what differences are the hardest to get past? Why?

- Do you notice yourself being quick to judge or quick to accept others? Why do you think that is?

- Ask God to bring to mind someone you leave out because she is different in some way. Hold her face in your mind and see what God may want to say to you about that person and how God may be inviting you to respond to that person.

[End]

TEMPLE OF GOD

Scripture References: Psalm 139:7-12; Isaiah 40:12-15; 1 Corinthians 3:16; 2 Corinthians 6:16

Theme: Presence of God

SNEAK PEEK

This exercise invites your students to reflect on the pervasive presence of God in their lives, that they are containers of the divine.

BELLS AND WHISTLES

- Imaginative Prayer Treasure Chest (refer to page 37)

- Posters or screen prompts displaying Psalm 139:7-11 or Isaiah 40:12-15

- Pictures that capture some of the imagery found in these verses

RUNDOWN

1. Slow Down (refer to page 44)

2. Read Imaginative Prayer Meditation (you'll read through the meditation three times). It's important for these words to begin to seep into the hearts of your students.

3. Offer students quiet space for reflection.

4. Optional Reflection/Journal Questions

IMAGINATIVE PRAYER MEDITATION

Think about God—how powerful God is; how big, how vast God is. Wherever you go, God is there. God is the Creator and Sustainer of all there was, is, and ever will be. Listen to these truths about God.

(Slowly read the two paragraphs below three times, pausing between each reading where indicated, before moving on to the next section.)

God is everywhere. Where can you go from God's Spirit? Where can you flee from God's presence? If you go up to the heavens, he is there; if you make your bed in the depths, he is there. If you rise on the wings of the dawn, if you settle on the far side of the sea, even there God's hand will guide you; God's right hand will hold you fast. God fills the heavens and the earth. God is HUGE. **(Pause a moment.)**

God has measured the waters in the hollow of his hand. God has marked off the heavens by the width of his hand. God has held the dust of the earth in a basket. God has weighed the mountains on the scales and the hills in a balance. The nations are like a drop in a bucket; they are regarded as dust on the scales; he weighs the islands as though they were fine dust. And we are like grasshoppers compared to God. **(Remember: Reread this section two more times before moving on.)**

Now try to imagine the hugeness, the bigness, the vastness of God. **(Pause a moment.)**

Keeping the immensity (hugeness) of God in mind, listen to these words of Paul: *You are the temple of God, the place where God hangs out and lives. You're the dwelling place of God. The God who is everywhere, the Creator of heaven and earth, the One who cannot be contained within the heavens, this God lives within you.* **(Pause a moment.)**

You are God's temple, God's dwelling place. Reflect upon this mystery. How does this feel? You're the dwelling place of God. God has chosen to live within you. Sit with that truth. God is not out there somewhere—God is in you. Inside of you God lives, moves, and has his being. Be still and ponder this mystery. God has chosen to take up residence in you.

OPTIONAL REFLECTION/JOURNAL QUESTIONS

- What feelings surfaced as you realized that God is always with you and that you're always with God?

- Does this bring you comfort, shame, fear, courage, strength, uneasiness? Why?

- How does thinking about God living within you make you feel?

- How might remembering that you're always in God's presence change how you live?

[End]

CHAPTER 14

BEYOND THE NARRATIVE
[SEVEN EXERCISES]

BLANKET WALK

Themes: Presence of God, Loved by God

SNEAK PEEK

Your students will be invited to wrap up in blankets and imaginatively experience being wrapped in God's love.

- Participants need their own blankets, one for each student.

- This is a two-phase exercise. The students will initially walk around while wrapped up in blankets, and then they'll be debriefed regarding their experiences.

- Then the students will once again walk around wrapped in blankets, but this time before they begin they'll be asked to imagine that the blanket is God's love. This second experience will then be debriefed as a group.

- This is an excellent exercise for a mild to cool day, and it's best experienced outside in nature. Doing this exercise in the mountains or on the beach works really well.

BELLS AND WHISTLES
- Imaginative Prayer Treasure Chest (refer to page 37)
- Blankets (provide them or ask your students to bring their own)

RUNDOWN
1. Make sure each student has a blanket.
2. Read Imaginative Prayer Meditation—Part One.

- When they return, debrief their experiences. See Optional Reflection/Journal Questions—Part One. You may wish to do this as a group.

- Read Imaginative Prayer Meditation—Part Two.

- Slow Down as indicated in meditation (refer to page 44)

- Release students.

- Offer students quiet space for reflection.

- Optional Reflection/Journal Questions—Part Two

IMAGINATIVE PRAYER MEDITATION—PART ONE

Wrap up in your blanket and walk around for a few minutes. **(Tell them when to return.)**

OPTIONAL REFLECTION/JOURNAL QUESTIONS—PART ONE

- What did it feel like to walk around that way? Why?

- What, if anything, did you like about it?

- What did you dislike about it?

IMAGINATIVE PRAYER MEDITATION—PART TWO

You're going to walk around wrapped in blankets one more time, but this time use your imagination. I want you to imagine you're not just wrapped up in a blanket; you're wrapped up in God's love. As you walk, sit, lie down, nap, or whatever it is you do, keep imagining you're wrapped in God's love. Notice how this makes you feel.

Before you head out, I'm going to lead you in a time of quieting down and opening up to God. When we're finished, please go in silence.

(Lead the students through the Slow Down, page 44. Afterward, send them out, but be sure to tell them when to return.)

OPTIONAL REFLECTION/JOURNAL QUESTIONS—PART TWO

- How was the first experience different from the second?

- Were you able to imagine that you were wrapped up in God's love? Was that difficult or easy for you to do? Why?

- What difference might it make if you truly believed God's love was always wrapped around you, no matter what?

- How might this affect how you see and feel about yourself?

[End]

BUBBLES

Themes: Freedom, Trust, Childlikeness

SNEAK PEEK

In this exercise the students will blow some bubbles. The bubbles help students learn what it means to live upon the currents of God's grace and the wings of God's Spirit. It also points to the fragility of life and how God is the author of life. It's a fairly free-flowing, imaginative experience. The key to this exercise is the debriefing time.

BELLS AND WHISTLES

- Imaginative Prayer Treasure Chest (refer to page 37)

- Different types of wands and a variety of containers to hold the bubble solution (plates, bowls, cups)

- Bubble machine (very cool!)

RUNDOWN

1. Your students will be blowing bubbles. This exercise is best done during the day when it's not too windy.

2. Each participant must have his own container of bubble soap and a wand. (Beware: Not all bubble solutions are created equally!)

3. Read Imaginative Prayer Meditation.

4. Send your students out.

5. Optional Reflection/Journal Questions. These are vital to the success of this exercise. We recommend you debrief as a group.

IMAGINATIVE PRAYER MEDITATION

As you read the Gospels, you discover that Jesus often used everyday things to teach people about God and about themselves. That's what we're going to do. Today we're going to blow some bubbles, and we're going to learn about God and ourselves while we do it. We'll learn from the bubbles and from each other.

In a minute, when we begin to blow bubbles, I want you to keep a couple of things in mind. The Bible tells us that God breathed life into humans. As you blow the bubbles, imagine God is breathing life into the bubbles. Then watch the bubbles after they detach from your wand. Where do they go? What do they look like? Are they all the same? Don't just blow the bubbles—*watch* the bubbles.

Also, in the Bible the word used for *spirit* is the same word used for *wind*. Keep this in mind and watch how the bubbles are impacted by the wind.

Some other things to experiment with: Try blowing hard, then try blowing softly. Notice the difference. Can you make the bubble go where you want it to go? Have fun and pay attention. God has some great things to teach us as we blow these bubbles. **(Pass out the bubbles, pray, and tell your students to have at it!)**

OPTIONAL REFLECTION/JOURNAL QUESTIONS

- What surprised you about this exercise?

- What happened if you blew too hard?

- How did the sun affect the appearance of the bubbles?

- How are bubbles like you?

- What do these bubbles teach you about yourself or about God?

- What do bubbles teach you about you *and* God?

- How is your life like the bubble on the wind?

- What keeps you from freely floating on the wind of God's Spirit?

[End]

THE FEAST

Theme: Significance

SNEAK PEEK

Your students experience themselves as the surprise guest of honor at a banquet hosted by Jesus. While at the banquet, the student sits next to Jesus, and Jesus makes a toast honoring her.

BELLS AND WHISTLES

- Imaginative Prayer Treasure Chest (refer to page 37)
- A long table set with a beautiful table cloth, real china, candles, cloth napkins, and so on
- Balloons and streamers hung around the room

RUNDOWN

1. Slow Down (refer to page 44)
2. Read Imaginative Prayer Meditation.
3. Display the words of the toast so your students can see it AFTER the exercise.
4. Offer students quiet space for reflection.
5. Optional Reflection/Journal Questions

IMAGINATIVE PRAYER MEDITATION

You are in a large room. There is a lot of activity as many people are busy making final preparations for a special event. The table is being set with silver, fine linen, beautiful flowers, and china. Yes, something very special is taking place. You can smell some wonderfully delicious smells coming from the kitchen.

But although you can see, hear, and even smell everything, you cannot be seen. You're an invisible observer, not part of these activities. Still, you can feel the great excitement in the room. The people who are setting the table, cooking the food, and arranging the flowers are all very excited.

You watch as Jesus enters the room; maybe all of this is for him. But he immediately joins in the work of getting everything ready. You watch as he carries in a big comfortable chair and places it at the head of the table. It's a beautiful chair with a high back and overstuffed cushions. All the other chairs around the table are plain wooden chairs. As Jesus puts the chair in its proper place, he announces that this is where the special guest will sit. You look on as everyone nods approval.

Who is the special guest? you wonder.

As you watch, the room is transformed before your very eyes, banners are hung, streamers are strung up, everything stands ready for the guest of honor. Those who've been helping momentarily disappear from the room, only to arrive a few minutes later all decked out in their best clothes. Soon other guests begin to arrive. The chairs around the table are filling up. In fact, with the arrival of these last two people, all the chairs are filled except for the big comfortable chair at the head of the table.

The guest of honor is due any minute.

Jesus peers out the front window and in an excited voice says, "Our special guest is on the way!" Jesus, unable to contain his excitement, begins to do a play-by-play, "I see our guest of honor walking up the street." Jesus quickly surveys the table, smiling with approval. He peers out the window and continues his play-by-play, "Our special guest is coming up the walkway. Now our special guest is standing on the porch. Our special guest is at the door!" The other guests giggle excitedly.

Jesus slowly opens the door as shouts and cheers of welcome from those around the table rain down on this special guest. Jesus leads the special guest to the place of honor, but you can't see who it is because Jesus' body is blocking your view. Then as Jesus moves to pull out the chair, you instantly recognize the guest. The guest is *you.*

Jesus is throwing a banquet for you! *You're* the special guest, the guest of honor. Jesus has arranged this all for you. As soon as Jesus helps you to your place, he moves to his place, which is right next to you, and proposes a toast.

While looking you in the eyes, Jesus raises his glass and says, "You are our special guest—my friend, the one I love, the one in whom I delight, and for whom I would rather die on a cross than live without. I pledge to you this day that I will never leave you nor forsake you, and my love will forever be poured out upon you. You are my friend, my chosen one, my beloved, special and unique in all the world."

OPTIONAL REFLECTION/JOURNAL QUESTIONS

* What was it like when you realized that you were to be the guest of honor?

- How did that realization make you feel?

- Do you think Jesus really feels that way about you? Why or why not?

- How do these words make you feel, "You are our special guest—my friend, the one I love, the one in whom I delight, and for whom I would rather die on a cross than live without. I pledge to you this day that I will never leave you nor forsake you, and my love will forever be poured out upon you. You are my friend, my chosen one, my beloved, special and unique in all the world."

- Were you able to receive and believe the words of Jesus? Why or why not?

- Do you believe you are "unique in all the world"? Why or why not?

[End]

THE LETTER

Theme: Honesty with God

SNEAK PEEK

This may be a new concept for your students. It has to do with the idea that we can express displeasure toward God and God is able to handle our raw honesty. God actually welcomes it. If you elect to do this exercise, it is important that you and your staff are comfortable with this concept.

This exercise has two parts. During the first part, the students write a letter to God. Then during the second part, you'll lead them through an imaginative exercise where they'll read their letters to God.

BELLS AND WHISTLES

- Imaginative Prayer Treasure Chest (refer to page 37)

- Paper and writing utensils

- Paper shredder

RUNDOWN

1. Read Imaginative Prayer Meditation—Part One.

2. Regroup.

3. Slow Down (refer to page 44)

4. Read Imaginative Prayer Meditation—Part Two.

5. Offer students quiet space for reflection.

6. Optional Reflection/Journal Questions

7. Allow your students the opportunity to dispose of their letter, if they wish.

IMAGINATIVE PRAYER MEDITATION—PART ONE

God wants our honesty, no matter how we feel or what we think. God, in fact, already knows what we're thinking and feeling deep inside. Being honest with God about difficult thoughts and feelings can bring healing and take away the power these thoughts and feelings have over us in terms of how we see ourselves, others, and God.

Two excellent biblical examples of this are—

- Jesus' crucifixion—when he cries out, "My God, my God, why have you forsaken me?" (in other words, "God, where did you go? Why did you leave me?"), and

- Jesus in the Garden of Gethsemane—when he expresses his honest desire to find a different way to complete his mission on earth, one that doesn't include the cross.

In both of these situations, Jesus was totally honest with God. If you add these examples to others we find in the Bible (including the Psalms, Moses, Job, and Jeremiah), it seems clear that God wants and welcomes our honesty.

Write a letter to God expressing the things in your life that are or have been hurtful, troubling, and difficult. No one else will read your letter. Write how these things make you feel about yourself and about God. Ask God any questions you have about these events, such as where was God when these things took place? Or why did these things have to happen?

After you've written the letter, go back over it one more time and ask yourself if there is anything you want to add or say in a stronger way. **(Allow your students to spread out to write their letters. Tell them when it's time to regroup. Then take them through the Slow Down, page 44, before moving on to part two.)**

IMAGINATIVE PRAYER MEDITATION—PART TWO

You're sitting at a large wooden desk. You lean back in your chair and reread the letter you've just written to God. You easily recall the pain of these circumstances you've written about. You allow yourself to feel whatever you're feeling. As you're reading over your letter, Jesus walks into the room. He takes a chair across the desk from you. He sits there silently for a few moments, and then he says, "I understand you wrote me a letter. Would you like to read it to me?" **(Pause a moment.)**

You slowly begin reading the letter to Jesus, looking up from time to time to see his expression, to look into his eyes, to see what he might be feeling as he sits and listens to every word. When you're finished, Jesus thanks you for your honesty and asks if there is anything else you would like to say. Jesus sits and waits for your response. **(Pause a moment.)**

Once you're finished, Jesus asks you to close your eyes. Then, after a few seconds, Jesus tells you to open your eyes. You open them and discover you're no longer behind the wooden desk. You're in a beautiful place. A place of comfort, safety, warmth, and beauty. You drink in your surroundings and feel yourself relax. You look at Jesus. His eyes communicate love, understanding, and sadness over what you've gone through and the struggles of your life. Now Jesus begins his response to you. What does Jesus say? Listen to his words and *beyond* his words—to his tone, his heart. Look deep within his eyes. What is Jesus saying to you?

OPTIONAL REFLECTION/JOURNAL QUESTIONS

- What was it like to write such an honest letter to God? How did you feel as you wrote it?

- What surprised you in your letter?

- How did Jesus receive your letter? What did you sense from Jesus as you read your letter?

- What did Jesus say to you after you shared your letter?

- What about Jesus' response surprised you? How was it said?

- How did Jesus' response make you feel about your letter? About yourself?

[End]

PLAYING IN THE LEAVES WITH DAD

Themes: Play, Childlikeness

SNEAK PEEK

God is not all seriousness. God created laughter and play. Sometimes we forget that. This exercise helps your students imagine God as a father who's inviting his child to play.

BELLS AND WHISTLES

- Imaginative Prayer Treasure Chest (refer to page 37)
- A big pile of leaves (it might be messy, but it's fun!)
- A rake
- A visual of trees in color

RUNDOWN

1. Slow Down (refer to page 44)
2. Read Imaginative Prayer Meditation.
3. Offer students quiet space for reflection.
4. Optional Reflection/Journal Questions

IMAGINATIVE PRAYER MEDITATION

It's Friday afternoon and you're walking home from school. The leaves are crunching under your feet. The breeze is slightly cool against your skin. It's been a long week. Actually, it's been a long semester. School has become really hard. Your classes are killing you, and there's tons of homework. You've had to drop most of the after-school stuff you used to do, just to keep up. It feels as though you haven't had a break in a long time. And you'll spend most of this weekend finishing up a huge class project.

The sun shines from behind a cloud and warms the air. It feels so good against your skin. Looking up toward the sky, you notice the trees lining your street. The leaves are in full color: yellows, oranges, and reds. You take a deep breath and release it. Your body begins to relax from all the effort of the past few weeks. You feel yourself smile.

Up ahead you see your house. Dad's in the front yard raking leaves. He's got a huge pile going. You realize it must be "yard work" day, and your smile begins to fade. He's going to ask you to help him, but you don't have time. You want to get right to work on that science project so you have plenty of time to do a good job. Your pace slows up as you near the driveway.

Dad looks up and sees you coming. He waves and calls out to you. "Hey there, do you mind giving me a little help?" You smile and wave, trying to look willing. He puts down his rake and runs over to you. He grabs your hand and you see he's got a big, silly grin on his face. "Ready. Set. Go!" he yells, and starts running back toward the house, still holding your hand. You run beside him, dropping your backpack along the way.

"Dad, what are you doing?" you yell.

"Jumping!" he calls back, and with that, he lets go of your hand, yells out "Woo hoo!" and jumps right into the pile of leaves. "Come on! Jump with me!" he shouts with that silly grin still plastered on his face. "It's fun!"

What do you want to do? What do you choose to do? **(Pause a moment.)**

Now consider this—Dad is actually God your Father. God knows all the work you have to do this weekend, but he also knows you need a break. You need to play. You haven't been playing nearly enough lately. So, as you near your home, God is outside raking the leaves into a big pile—I mean a REALLY big pile. Take a moment to re-enter the scene. **(Pause a moment.)**

When God, your Dad, sees you coming, he waves and calls out to you, "Hey there, do you mind giving me a little help?" You smile and wave, trying to look willing. He puts down his rake and runs over to you. He grabs your hand and you see he's got a big, silly grin on his face. "Ready. Set. Go!" he yells, and starts running back toward the house, still holding your hand. You run beside him, dropping your backpack along the way.

"Dad, what are you doing?" you yell.

"Jumping!" he calls back, and with that, he lets go of your hand, yells out "Woo hoo!" and jumps right into the pile of leaves. "Come on! Jump with me!" he shouts with that silly grin still plastered on his face. "It's fun!"

What do you want to do? What do you choose to do?

OPTIONAL REFLECTION/JOURNAL QUESTIONS

- How do you usually feel when you play? Why?

- How do you think God feels when you play? Why?

- Since God created play, what does that say about who God is? What does that say about the value of playing?

- How does knowing that God created play make you feel about God?

- How does knowing that God created play make you feel about playing?

[End]

HIDE-AND-SEEK

Scripture References: Psalm 139:1-4, 7-10; Matthew 18:3; Acts 17:28; Colossians 3:3

Themes: Presence of God, Childlikeness

SNEAK PEEK

During this exercise the students will play a game of hide-and-seek with God, which will show them they can't hide from God, and they'll be asked to interact with this truth.

BELLS AND WHISTLES

- Imaginative Prayer Treasure Chest (refer to page 37)

- Crayons and paper for drawing pictures

- A few toys and stuffed animals scattered around the room

RUNDOWN

1. Read Imaginative Prayer Meditation.

2. Pass out the following three-by-five cards to each student. (You'll want to photocopy them beforehand. Cardstock would be a good paper choice.) Each time the students hide during the game, they'll read their three cards.

CARD 1

MY CHILD, YOU CANNOT HIDE FROM ME.

Where can I go from your Spirit? Where can I flee from your presence? If I go up to the heavens, you are there; if I make my bed in the depths, you are there. If I rise on the wings of the dawn, if I settle on the far side of the sea, even there your hand will guide me, your right hand will hold me fast. (Psalm 139:7-10)

CARD 2

MY PRECIOUS LITTLE ONE, I KNOW YOU SO WELL AND I LOVE YOU SO DEEPLY. YOU CANNOT HIDE FROM ME.

O LORD, you have searched me and you know me. You know when I sit and when I rise; you perceive my thoughts from afar. You discern my going out and my lying down; you are familiar with all my ways. Before a word is on my tongue you know it completely, O LORD. (Psalm 139:1-4)

CARD 3

MY DELIGHTFUL CHILD—YOU MAKE ME LAUGH WITH JOY. YOU CANNOT HIDE FROM ME.

For you died, and your life is now hidden with Christ in God. (Colossians 3:3)

For in him we live and move and have our being. (Acts 17:28)

1. Slow Down as indicated in the meditation (refer to page 44).

2. Start counting to 50 and send the students out to hide and silently read their cards in each of their hiding spots.

3. After the game ends, invite your students to draw a picture representing their experience.

4. Offer students quiet space for reflection.

5. Optional Reflection/Journal Questions

IMAGINATIVE PRAYER MEDITATION

(Read aloud Matthew 18:3.) Jesus encourages us to become like children, so that's what we'll be doing for the next several minutes. We're going to play a game of hide-and-seek. In a bit, I'll instruct you to hide. As soon as I start counting, get up and find a place to hide. You won't be hiding from me. You'll be hiding from God. We're going to play hide-and-seek with God.

First I'll give you three cards, but don't look at them yet. I'm going to start by leading you through a slowing-down process to help you prepare for this exercise. Then this is how it'll work. I'll start counting and you exit quietly and find a place to hide. Settle into your place, remain quiet, and try not to move. When you feel settled and calm, read the first card—let the words sink in and reflect on how the words make you feel. Don't hurry.

When you're finished, move to another hiding spot, sit quietly, and read your second card. Remember to take your time. Continue playing hide-and-seek until you're finished with all three cards. Then return here and draw a picture about your experience.

(Begin the Slow Down on page 44. Once you've finished, start counting...you may have to remind your students to go hide.)

OPTIONAL REFLECTION/JOURNAL QUESTIONS

- What was it like to play hide-and-seek with God?

- Which of the cards did you like the best? Why? What words on that card seemed most important for you to hear? Why?

- Has God ever come seeking you? If so, how did it happen? What did it feel like? What did you do in response? Did this seeking change you in any way?

- Where do you hide from God? You might want to write a letter and ask God to tell you about your hiding places.

- Spend some time thinking about how God is always with you. There's nowhere to hide from God. Does this bring a sense of comfort or discomfort?

- Reflect upon your feelings and the "why" behind them. Allow this to lead you into a time of prayer.

[End]

SUNRISE

Themes: Praise, Joy, Significance

SNEAK PEEK

In this exercise God invites your students to watch a sunrise, a gift God has made for each of them. It's an invitation to worship.

BELLS AND WHISTLES

- Imaginative Prayer Treasure Chest (refer to page 37)

- A blanket for every student

- Darkened room with sunrise visual shown at the end of the exercise

- Ocean and/or wind sounds

RUNDOWN

1. Slow Down (refer to page 44)

2. Read Imaginative Prayer Meditation.

3. Offer students quiet space for reflection.

4. Optional Reflection/Journal Questions

IMAGINATIVE PRAYER MEDITATION

You awaken, shivering in the darkness. A voice asks you to come along and wraps a warm blanket around you when you stand. God holds your hand and guides you out the door and down the steps. A cold blast of wind hits your face and you pull the blanket more tightly around you.

You walk without seeing, trusting the One who leads you. "Here," God says, "let's sit down." You sit; and since you can't see anything, you listen. You hear the wind in the trees behind you and the ocean far below.

"Why are we here?" you ask.

"I made you something," God answers. "Look." You do, and you can see the sky getting lighter and a rainbow of colors filling every corner of it—hues of pink, orange, yellow, blue, and purple. The morning is being born, re-created once again. God's voice speaks, "A new day, a new hope, and a new beginning for you."

The ocean down below begins to sparkle and shine, while the clouds above radiate with color. The sun breaks dramatically over the horizon. The waves crash, the wind blows, and the birds begin their morning song.

All of creation praises God and you feel your heart begin to sing, too. You turn to look at God, who is already looking at you. God smiles and asks, "Do you like it?"

Sit in awe of your Creator God, the One who dreamed and formed this world, the One who dreamed and formed you. Join the rest of creation in praise of the One who was, is, and always will be.

OPTIONAL REFLECTION/JOURNAL QUESTIONS

- What was your experience like as you watched the sunrise with God? Share your heart with God. Feel free to thank God for anything that brings you joy—like a sunrise.

- Do you need a new beginning, a fresh start? You're invited to talk to God about your desire for a new day.

- How does it feel to consider that God made the sunrise just for you?

- In the exercise, God asked if you liked the sunrise. How did that make you feel?

- Do you think God wants to please you with gifts? Why or why not?

[End]

GET CREATIVE! MORE IMAGINATIVE PRAYER IDEAS

In this appendix, we've listed a sampling of ideas to encourage your students to experience God through their imaginations. Check them out. You can use them in conjunction with the exercises in this book or in whatever capacity you choose. Use them as they're written or as starting points to help you create your own ideas. Be yourself. Be creative. You were made to be both.

PRAYER POSTURES

We can actually pray with our bodies. Encourage your students to move into a position that wordlessly expresses their hearts to God. Try this after a guided meditation or after slowly and thoughtfully reading a passage of Scripture. Or speak a single word at a time, asking them to respond to whichever word(s) draws them with a posture that expresses their feelings to God. Ask your students to notice what's going on for them in this exercise. Are they hesitant to participate? Do they feel free enough to express themselves with their bodies? How are they impacted by noticing those around them?

ACTION FIGURES

You can provide action figures or dolls and invite your students to choose one. Follow the same instructions given above for prayer postures, but use these action figures instead. It can feel less vulnerable for a person to move around a doll instead of moving one's own body, yet it can still be a powerful prayer experience for your students.

ROLE-PLAY

Divide your students into groups and give them a biblical narrative to act out. Assign them roles or have them choose their own. Then read the narrative from the front of the room and have your students close their eyes and listen, imaginatively entering the setting as their chosen character.

Read the narrative a second time, slowly, pausing after each action in the story. Then have each group role-play the narrative, with each student participating in the scene.

Read the scene a third time, and ask the students to imaginatively enter the scene again, noticing what draws them or repels them. Give them individual debriefing time to sit with their emotions and experiences and come before God with them. Then ask if some students would like to share what it was like to be their character.

ALTARS

Build an altar with objects that will capture the imagination of your students. Consider both contemporary and traditional symbols. Use candles, crosses, or crucifixes. Use images. Use elements that include the senses. You may choose a specific theme or passage of Scripture to inspire the altar creation. Provide materials so your students can create their own altars, or divide them into smaller groups. Let each group choose a theme for their altar and let them loose. You can create altars that will last for one meeting or for a season. Perhaps you can even get permission to have your students create an altar for the main worship area of your church building.

PRAYER STATIONS

Prayer stations can be kept available long-term or used for just one meeting. They can reflect a theme or a season. You can create prayer stations yourself or empower your students to make their own.

Make use of the senses and let them draw or paint or blow bubbles. Have them write a love note to God or to themselves from God. Allow them to take a journey through the Stations of the Cross, or create a manger and allow your students to sit before the Christ child. Let them smell fragrant oil that was poured from a jar to anoint Jesus. Invite them to lie on cushions and rest with Jesus in the midst of a storm. Have them light a candle and pray for those who are marginalized, oppressed, and vulnerable.

Prayer stations can be used as the primary imaginative prayer element or as a way to individually debrief an imaginative prayer exercise. A person can linger at a prayer station for an hour or just stop there for two minutes. They work well for students with differing attention spans and for various time constraints as well.

BEYOND THE NARRATIVE

What about imaginative prayer meditations that aren't pulled from Scripture? We believe any setting where a person is given an opportunity to encounter God can become prayer. It can be transformational to imaginatively meet Jesus in an empty, quiet meadow. We can experience healing when we allow God to imaginatively rock us in big loving arms as we cry and share our grief. We may begin to feel beautiful when we look into a mirror with God, allowing God to tell us what God sees. We can find the courage to keep walking when we picture God walking at our side. We've included several extrabiblical meditations in chapter 14 of this book, so check those out and make up your own mind.

BIBLE VERSIONS

The Bible is story, and we become engaged in that story when it touches something in our imagination. As you introduce a Scripture passage to your students, consider what translation works best for them. Look at the different choices. If you tend to use a particular version, try a new one and see if a different wording gives the narrative a fresh feel for you and your students. Read dramatically or very slowly. Or allow them to read silently to themselves. You may even want to paraphrase the passage. Make it current-day if you want. Make the language understandable and approachable for your students. If they're going to imaginatively enter a story, they need to easily understand it. They need to be able to relate to it.

STORIES

Short stories, children's stories, and excerpts from books can be a great aid in helping your students explore, embrace, and experience powerful biblical themes or familiar biblical stories in a new way. Choose stories and books that draw you into the narrative by their creative use of words or the vivid mental pictures their words call forth.

Consider using the two sections from C. S. Lewis' Chronicles of Narnia series where he describes Aslan's death and Aslan's return to life. Merely reading C. S. Lewis' words to your students to encourage them to enter into the story will touch many of them in new ways regarding Jesus' death and resurrection.

Think back through stories you're familiar with, ones that communicate biblical truth in creative ways. Pass out blankets or pillows (or ask people to bring their own) so they can get cozy while you read to them. It really helps them relax, listen, and enter into the story more fully. Reading to your students is an excellent way to help them rediscover their imaginations and move them from head to heart knowledge.

MOVIE CLIPS

Like story, the use of movie clips can be powerful. Your students live in a visual world, so using movie clips connects with where they live. And films can communicate powerful biblical truths and themes. The use of images, color, and music combined together in a movie clip can make a very big impact.

Larry adds a word of caution:

> *I admit I've never used a movie clip in imaginative prayer. I'm cautious about movies for meditation exercises because students are so used to that medium. I opt for silence or reading a narrative. I prefer something that they don't normally experience. BUT I also know personally that God can speak powerfully through the movies.*

FINGER PAINTS

Using finger paints allows your students to escape the confines of words and express themselves through the medium of color and paint. You can use finger paints in conjunction with music, spoken words (words that God uses to describe your students, God's words of promise and hope, and so on), or spoken narrative. This can free your students to express beyond words what they internally experience of themselves and God.

Pass out a large piece of newsprint, and give each student a variety of colors (happy, sad, angry, and calm colors). Invite your students to express what they're feeling through finger paint as they listen. Play music, read a biblical narrative, or speak individual words of love, longing, pain, brokenness, or belonging. Allow your students to express themselves.

BLINDFOLDED FINGER PAINTING

Give your students a blindfold, a large piece of newsprint, and two or three colors of finger paint. Lead them into prayer where they'll speak to God without words, but through the use of movement and colors on the newsprint. Invite them to express themselves to God from a place beyond words, trusting the Holy Spirit to communicate to God what they're seeking to express. The blindfolds help diminish distractions and performance issues.

BODY BAGS

Is that a typo? No, it's not. Larry explains:

> *I've been deeply impacted by the use of body bags. It helped me get a sense of being dead in trespasses and sins and then coming to life in Christ. The body bags were not just a visual prop. I got into one and zipped it up. It was a sobering experience—imagining what death would be like and the importance of living today. Body bags can be used to help students embrace a number of biblical truths, but be aware that this can be a very intense experience. Simply looking at body bags or photos of death can bring up very strong feelings. Please be cautious with this idea; make sure you let your supervisor (and maybe parents) know ahead of time if you want to try it.*

ROCKS

We're big fans of rocks. They can be used in a number of ways. Rocks can symbolize burdens, sins, personal struggles, and so on. Have your students hold a rock and imagine that it contains all their pain. Invite them to drop the rock into a bucket of water, throw it into a lake, or place it at the foot of a cross—symbolically and imaginatively placing their pain into God's hands.

You could have a pile of rocks, where each one represents a burden. Your students can be invited to choose from these rocks, place them into their backpacks, and physically carry their burdens during your time together. Then every once in a while, stop what you're doing and invite your students to remove a rock from their backpacks. Ask them to feel the weight and texture of the rock and to tell God what it represents. Invite them to offer this rock and what it symbolizes to God. Repeat this throughout your time together.

COLLAGE

Here's a debriefing idea. Collaging (new word) is a great way to debrief individually and as a group. After an imaginative exercise, have the students go through magazines (you do have a bunch of magazines in your treasure chest, don't you?) and cut or tear out pictures or words that convey what they felt and experienced about themselves, Jesus, others—whatever you decide. They can do this individually, but then at the end you may want to create a giant collage bringing together your students' words and pictures.

LABYRINTHS AND MAZES

Labyrinths are different from mazes. Mazes have lots of paths and mostly dead ends. You can get lost in a maze. You can choose incorrectly. Mazes are about strategy, while labyrinths, which predate mazes, have only one path. This path leads to the center and back out again. Labyrinths can help us reflect on our journey with God.

You may have access to a walking labyrinth at a nearby church. If so, consider taking your kids through it. You can create your own, although it takes some commitment. There are books and Web sites dedicated to creating labyrinths. To outline the path and perimeters you can use tape or chalk or something more permanent. Or consider this simple idea: Print out a labyrinth on paper and invite students to use a pencil or their finger to travel the labyrinth. Printable labyrinths are easily found via Internet searches as well.

Whether you use a walking labyrinth or a finger labyrinth, encourage your students to slowly journey to the center of the labyrinth, quieting themselves on the way and listening for God's whisper. They may wish to stay in the center for some period of time and just "be" with God. Invite them to imaginatively walk out of the center, allowing God to accompany them in their journey back out into the world.

Another idea is to print up some mazes and some labyrinths on paper. Here are a couple of Web pages to check out: The Maze Generator at www.billsgames.com/mazegenerator and the Mazes page at www.mazes.org.uk.

Allow your students to try a difficult maze and reflect on their feelings. Then allow them to journey through a labyrinth. Invite them to travel along this path with Jesus, reflecting on their lives and his involvement in their journey. Give them time to consider the difference between their experiences with the maze and the labyrinth.

ADDITIONAL RESOURCES

- *Elements Volume One: Moving Images for Worship* CD-ROM by Highway Visual (YS/Zondervan, 2004)

- *Elements Volume Two: Moving Images for Worship* CD-ROM by Highway Visual (YS/Zondervan, 2004)

- *Elements Volume Three: Moving Images for Worship* CD-ROM by Highway Visual (YS/Zondervan, 2005)

- *Elements Volume Four: Moving Images for Worship* CD-ROM by Highway Visual (YS/Zondervan, 2005)

- *Every Picture Tells a Story: 48 Evocative Photographs for Inspiring Reaction and Reflection* by Mark Oestreicher (YS/Zondervan, 2002)

- *Worship Image Gallery on CD-ROM: 700 Photos and Digital Artwork for Visual Churches* (YS/Zondervan, 2003)

INDEX BY SCRIPTURE REFERENCE

GENESIS

16:6-13   God Sees Hagar, 61

EXODUS

19:4   God as Eagle, 52

NUMBERS

24:17   Names (Images) of Jesus, 80

DEUTERONOMY

32:10-11   God as Eagle, 52

1 SAMUEL

1:1-28   Hannah's Cry, 63

1 KINGS

18:30-40;

19:1-7   Elijah Rests and Eats, 64

19:8-13   God Whispers to Elijah, 67

ESTHER

1–10   Esther's Courage, 68

PSALMS

Various   The Desperate Cry, 70

18   God as Rescuer, 57

23   God as Shepherd, 59

57:1   God as Eagle, 52

131   God as Mother, 54

139:1-4, 7-10   Hide-and-Seek, 157

139:7-12   Temple of God, 144

ISAIAH

7:14	Names (Images) of Jesus, 80
9:6	Names (Images) of Jesus, 80
40:12-15	Temple of God, 144
62:1-12	A New Name, 72
64:8	God as Potter, 55
66:13	God as Mother, 54

DANIEL

6:1-28	Daniel and the Lions' Den, 73
7:9	Names (Images) of Jesus, 80

ZEPHANIAH

3:17	God as Mother, 54

ZECHARIAH

9:9	Names (Images) of Jesus, 80

MATTHEW

1:23	Names (Images) of Jesus, 80; God with Us, 83
6:9-15	The Lord's Prayer, 85
7:21-23	"I Never Knew You", 88
11:19	Names (Images) of Jesus, 80
11:28-30	Rest, 90
12:18	Names (Images) of Jesus, 80
14:22-27	Jesus Walks on Water, 115
14:22-32	Peter Walks on Water, 117
16:13-16	"Who Do You Say I Am?" (Jesus), 93; "Who Do You Say I Am?" (Us), 96
18:3	Hide-and-Seek, 157
26:36-44	Garden of Gethsemane, 136
27:11-66	The Crucifixion, 138
28:20	God with Us, 83

MARK

1:24	Names (Images) of Jesus, 80
4:35-41	Jesus Calms the Storm,120; Resting with Jesus, 122
5:25-34	She Touches His Robe, 125
8:29	Names (Images) of Jesus, 80
10:13-16	Coming to Jesus, 98
10:46-52	The Blind Beggar, 127
14:3-9	Woman with the Alabaster Jar, 100

LUKE

1:26-38	Mary's Pregnant, 76
1:78	Names (Images) of Jesus, 80
2:8-20	Shepherds in the Field, 78
5:12-13	Healing the Leper, 129
5:16	The Lord's Prayer, 85
10:30-37	Good Samaritan, 102
10:38-42	Martha, 103
15:11-24	The Prodigal, 105
18:15-17	Coming to Jesus, 98

JOHN

1:1	Names (Images) of Jesus, 80
1:29	Names (Images) of Jesus, 80
1:29-38	John's Disciple Follows Jesus, 108
4:42	Names (Images) of Jesus, 80
6:35	Names (Images) of Jesus, 80
8:1-11	Woman Caught in Adultery, 110
8:12	Names (Images) of Jesus, 80
8:58	Names (Images) of Jesus, 80
10:9	Names (Images) of Jesus, 80
10:11	Names (Images) of Jesus, 80
11:1-35	Death of Lazarus, 113
11:1-44	Resurrection of Lazarus, 132
11:25	Names (Images) of Jesus, 80
13:1-5	Foot Washing, 134

14:6	Names (Images) of Jesus, 80
15:1	Names (Images) of Jesus, 80
15:13-14	Names (Images) of Jesus, 80
19:1-42	The Crucifixion, 138
20:28	Names (Images) of Jesus, 80

ACTS

| 10:1-48 | Peter and Cornelius, 142 |
| 17:28 | Hide-and-Seek, 157 |

1 CORINTHIANS

| 3:16 | Temple of God, 144 |
| 10:4 | Names (Images) of Jesus, 80 |

2 CORINTHIANS

| 6:16 | Temple of God, 144 |
| 9:15 | Names (Images) of Jesus, 80 |

COLOSSIANS

| 3:3 | Hide-and-Seek, 157 |

HEBREWS

| 13:5 | God with Us, 83 |
| 4:14-16 | Garden of Gethsemane, 136 |

REVELATION

19:13	Names (Images) of Jesus, 80
22:13	Names (Images) of Jesus, 80
22:16	Names (Images) of Jesus, 80

INDEX BY THEME

ACCEPTANCE The Prodigal, 105; Healing the Leper, 129

BEING VERSUS DOING "I Never Knew You", 88

CHILDLIKENESS Bubbles, 148; Playing in the Leaves with Dad, 155; Hide-and-Seek, 157

COMFORTED God as Mother, 54

COMPASSION Death of Lazarus, 113; Healing the Leper, 129

CONFUSION God as Eagle, 52; God Whispers to Elijah, 67

COURAGE Esther's Courage, 68; Daniel and the Lions' Den, 73; Woman with the Alabaster Jar, 100; She Touches His Robe, 125

DEPRESSION Elijah Rests and Eats, 64

DESIRE Coming to Jesus, 98; Woman with the Alabaster Jar, 100; John's Disciple Follows Jesus, 108; The Blind Beggar, 127

FAILURE Peter Walks on Water, 117

FAITH Hannah's Cry, 63; Mary's Pregnant, 76; Jesus Walks on Water, 115; She Touches His Robe, 125; The Blind Beggar, 127

FEAR Elijah Rests and Eats, 64; Jesus Calms the Storm, 120

FORGIVENESS The Prodigal, 105; Woman Caught in Adultery, 110

FREEDOM Bubbles, 148

GOD'S CARE God as Shepherd, 59

GRACE The Prodigal, 105

GRIEF Death of Lazarus, 113; The Crucifixion, 138

GUIDANCE God Whispers to Elijah, 67

GUILT Woman Caught in Adultery, 110

HEALING She Touches His Robe, 125

HONESTY Hannah's Cry, 63; The Desperate Cry, 70

HONESTY WITH GOD Garden of Gethsemane, 136; The Letter 152

IDENTITY God as Rescuer, 57; A New Name, 72; "Who Do You Say I Am?" (Us), 96

IMAGES OF JESUS Names (Images) of Jesus, 80; "Who Do You Say I Am?" (Jesus), 93

JOY   Shepherds in the Field, 78; Sunrise, 160

JUSTICE   Esther's Courage, 68

LONELINESS   Coming to Jesus, 98

LOVE FOR GOD   Daniel and the Lions' Den, 73

LOVED BY GOD   God as Mother, 54; God as Potter, 55; God as Rescuer, 57; A New Name, 72; Woman with the Alabaster Jar, 100; Martha, 103; Blanket Walk, 146

LOVING OTHERS   Good Samaritan, 102; Peter and Cornelius, 142

PEACE   God as Shepherd, 59; Resting with Jesus, 122

PLAY   Playing in the Leaves with Dad, 155

POWER   Resurrection of Lazarus, 132

POWERLESSNESS   God Sees Hagar, 61; The Desperate Cry, 70

PRAISE   Sunrise, 160

PRAYER   The Lord's Prayer, 85

PRESENCE OF GOD   God with Us, 83; Temple of God, 144; Blanket Walk, 146; Hide-and-Seek, 157

RESCUE   God as Eagle, 52; God as Rescuer, 57; God Sees Hagar, 61

REST   God as Mother, 54; Elijah Rests and Eats, 64; Rest, 90; Resting with Jesus, 122

SAFETY   God as Shepherd, 59

SHAME   Woman Caught in Adultery, 110

SIGNIFICANCE   God as Potter, 55; A New Name, 72; Shepherds in the Field, 78; Martha, 103; Foot Washing, 134; The Feast, 150; Sunrise, 160

SIN   Woman Caught in Adultery, 110

SUFFERING   The Desperate Cry, 70

TRUST   God as Eagle, 52; Daniel and the Lions' Den, 73; Coming to Jesus, 98; Jesus Walks on Water, 115; Peter Walks on Water, 117; Resting with Jesus, 122; Bubbles, 148

WORRIES   Elijah Rests and Eats, 64